Frontispiece

# Tales of a New England Boyhood

## Scituate, Massachusetts 1931-1946

by
Donald E. Hattin

Bloomington, IN  Milton Keynes, UK

*AuthorHouse™*
*1663 Liberty Drive, Suite 200*
*Bloomington, IN 47403*
*www.authorhouse.com*
*Phone: 1-800-839-8640*

*AuthorHouse™ UK Ltd.*
*500 Avebury Boulevard*
*Central Milton Keynes, MK9 2BE*
*www.authorhouse.co.uk*
*Phone: 08001974150*

© 2006 Donald E. Hattin. All rights reserved.

*No part of this book may be reproduced, stored in a retrieval system, or transmitted by any means without the written permission of the author.*

*First published by AuthorHouse 7/21/2006*

*ISBN: 1-4259-4245-8 (sc)*
*ISBN: 1-4259-4248-2 (dj)*

*Printed in the United States of America*
*Bloomington, Indiana*

*This book is printed on acid-free paper.*

# Dedication

With love and admiration, I dedicate this bit of American history to my children; Sandy, Ron, and Donna; to my grandsons, Whitney and Alan; and to my granddaughter, Devin. Their questions have served as inspiration and I hope that in this book they find some of the answers.

# Table of Contents

Dedication .......................................................................................... v

Foreword ......................................................................................... ix

Acknowledgments............................................................................ xi

Chapter 1: Scituate Boyhood: An "Old Man's" Perspective . 1

Chapter 2: Una Whipple Hattin ................................................. 4

Chapter 3: 612 Country Way ..................................................... 19

Chapter 4: The Barn.................................................................... 40

Chapter 5: Hatherly School........................................................ 50

Chapter 6: North Scituate Beach And Beyond ..................... 75

Chapter 7: Construction Projects ............................................ 88

Chapter 8: Family Outings And Other Travels ................... 103

Chapter 9: Grandparents ........................................................... 120

Chapter 10: Aunt Millie And Uncle Bud .............................. 135

Chapter 11: Around The Neighborhood............................... 147

Chapter 12: Apples, Sea Moss, And Other Odd Jobs ......... 203

Chapter 13: Scouting Adventures ........................................... 215

Chapter 14: North Scituate A&P Store ................................. 244

Chapter 15: Lobster Fishing...................................................... 258

Chapter 16: First Baptist Church And A Close Call ........... 264

Chapter 17: Sentimental Journey ....................................... 271

Chapter 18: Ben Meyers' Farm .......................................... 280

Chapter 19: Secondary School ........................................... 293

Chapter 20: End Of The Beginning ................................... 314

# Foreword

As the 20th century neared its end, I found myself reflecting ever more frequently on the happy circumstances of my boyhood, remembering with crystal clarity details of events which profoundly affected all of my later years. My childhood and youth were doubtlessly no more remarkable than those of my schoolmates, and may have been less so, but were certainly filled to the brim with variety, challenge, inquiry, and adventure. At the age of five, I was already involved in mischievous, even perilous schemes, and could hardly wait to begin each day's exciting activities, school included! Looking back, my youthful exuberance seems to have been nearly boundless. With rare exceptions, I was never bored – there were too many things to do, too many places to be explored, too much happening in the neighborhood, and too much to learn. These are reasons enough to commit my recollections to paper, thus sharing them with my children, grandchildren, boyhood friends, and those whose interest is piqued by the title of this modest volume.

My book is not to be regarded as an autobiography, although much of its content may appear to be such. An autobiography progresses chronologically through a writer's life, but *Tales of a New England Boyhood* is instead a series of essays, each comprising a chapter concerned with specific subject matter, including stories about people, places, events or activities with whom or with which I was involved.

Chapters are arranged in a generally chronologic sequence, but many of the "tales" overlap the time frame of others. For example, the chapter relating to scouting experiences embraces almost the same time interval as that concerned with secondary school.

Overlapping chronology aside, I hope that this will be viewed as a contribution to the history of Scituate, 1931-1946, from the perspective of one who, in a very small way, helped to create that history.

Bloomington, IN, April, 2006

# Acknowledgments

Several of my grade school and high school friends gave generously of their time, their recollections of events, and photographic resources, thus adding materially to the substance of this book. Ward Cobb "Cobby" Swift furnished the only known photograph of the old beachwagon which we called "the jeep," several slides pertaining to Scituate Boy Scout Troop 5, a photograph of our second grade class at Hatherly School, and a photograph of the 1946 class of Scituate High School graduates. Edward "Punch" Swift sent information concerning construction of our scout cabin at the so-called "Mill Pond." Gray Curtis furnished a photo of the former Curtis Home Bakery bakeshop, gave freely of his knowledge regarding bakery history, and assisted with research in the Scituate Historical Society archives. Madeline Riani Barry thoughtfully sent the image of herself, me, and my two sisters. Paul "P" Miles sent historic details concerning Lawson Tower and the First Baptist Church in North Scituate, and succeeded in tracking down a photograph featuring Sidney Gates' dry goods store and the A&P store in North Scituate Village. That photo was presented by Lawrence "Chick" Gates, one of Sidney's sons. Carol Miles graciously arranged for the loan of several images from files of the Scituate Historical Society, and dug up genealogical material about Jeremiah Ainslie. Alfred "Monty" Montanari sent information regarding his brother, Arthur, and about his own service in the U.S. Marine Corps during WWII. Laurianne Olcott of Rumney, NH, granddaughter of Bernard Meyers and daughter of Ben's son, Elden, kindly searched her family's archives, located several photos pertaining to Ben's farm, and sent copies to me via e-mail. To each of these friends, without whose help this book would lack important details, I offer heartfelt gratitude.

DeAnn Reinhart, Department of Geological Sciences, Indiana University, prepared all drafts of the typescript, starting with my completely henscratched manuscript. Many, many thanks, DeAnn. Barbara Hill and John Day of the Indiana Geological Survey scanned all of the original photographs and photocopies, digitally enhanced those in need of clarification, and prepared for publication a CD containing all of the images incorporated herein. Their fine work has done much to improve the quality of this volume, and will be gratefully remembered. Finally, I wish to extend sincerest thanks for the continued encouragement of all who knew that this work was in progress. To each of them, and especially my wife Margie, I extend my profoundest thanks.

# Chapter 1
## Scituate Boyhood: An "Old Man's" Perspective

As a white-haired septuagenarian, I reflect with growing pleasure and amusement on the good fortune of having experienced boyhood in such a historic and endlessly fascinating place as Scituate, Massachusetts. There, in the 1930's and early to mid-1940's, the pace of life was slower than at present, technological distractions were few, and childhood friendships were destined to endure well into the succeeding century. I look back with more than a little nostalgia to a time when folks in general hued to higher moral and ethical standards than at present. Respect for one's elders was universal, teenage "crime" consisted of occasionally tipping over an outhouse, and drug abuse was unheard of. Some movies were scary and some were thrilling, but none was drenched in sex, violence and foul language. Workers young and old, male and female, put in an honest day's work, and loyalty to one's employer was a given. Gentlemen removed their hats when indoors, tipped those hats to passing ladies, helped the latter on and off with their coats, and politely held doors open when those of the fairer gender were entering or leaving a building. Many contracts were sealed with a handshake, and litigation over the tiniest of transgressions was a societal malady still far in the future. Doctors routinely made house calls, and affixed atop their car license plates the green emblem of their profession. Everyone dressed for church, coats and ties being de rigueur for men, and the ladies wore hats. Getting married and raising a family is what nearly all young people planned to do and is what nearly all of them did. Most moms were just that – moms. Raising children and keeping house was a full-time job. World War II brought town and country together in ways seen neither before nor since. Nearly everyone participated in the war effort – serving in the armed forces, participating in scrap drives, serving as aircraft spotters, training for emergencies, and willingly accepting the need for food and gasoline rationing.

Kids in my school classes seemed never to have a "hangup," and if they did, it certainly escaped my notice. Besides, there was no buzzword to describe such a situation and no obvious whining about it. Come to think of it, only one grade-school boy of my acquaintance might have been put on a tranquilizer had he lived in the 1990's instead of the 1930's. Still and all, he was not a bad kid, no one disliked him, and so far as I know he was only paddled once by our principal. With possible exception of small pocket knives, "weapons" as we know them today were *never* brought to school and not one of my friends would ever have considered doing so. School kids didn't deface their books (which were furnished for free by the town), and obeyed rules which were so obvious that they didn't require articulation. To the "liberated" kids of the past three decades, all of the foregoing may seem pretty restrictive, but we were hardly submissive, and in the end our high school graduating class went on to live useful and productive lives which contributed in many valuable ways to the fabric of American society. Members of our class became successful in business, engineering, research, education, nursing, law enforcement, the trades and more. And why not? We are the grateful beneficiaries of traditional upbringing, a solid no-nonsense educational system, and communities of friendly neighbors. Most of what we have accomplished in life is owing to the encouraging environment afforded by a small town situated on the Atlantic seaboard in a county founded by the Mayflower pilgrims. They had much for which to be thankful, and so do we.

# Chapter 2
## Una Whipple Hattin

My mother, "Mama" as she was called during my childhood, was the dominant force in my boyhood, and worked ceaselessly to ensure that our upbringing was of the highest possible standard. She could be firm when necessary, and strict as occasion demanded, but she had a great sense of humor, a strong social conscience, and a heart made of solid gold. She had many talents, and shared these freely.

Born in Philadelphia on July 19, 1897, and named Una Vestella Whipple, she lived most of her girlhood in Diamond Hill, RI, and adjacent West Wrentham, MA, and attended grade schools in that area. Next enrolling in a private prep school, she graduated from Dean Academy, Franklin, MA, in 1915, and proceeded thence to Pembroke College of Brown University, from which she received an A.B. degree in 1919. Following college, she taught (1919-1921) in Clark School for the Deaf, Northampton, MA, and later, after she married my father, in the Horace Mann School in Boston (1921-1922). Her professional

*Tales of a New England Boyhood*

Una Whipple Hattin, ca. 1924.

career ended with arrival of her children, but she was an astute and patient teacher until life's end.

When I was only 4 years old, I found out about footballs, and I remember hollering, "I want a football, I want a football!" So, Mom got me a football. Just how I learned about football remains a mystery because neither parent was a sports fan, I had never seen a football game, and I most certainly did not read the sports pages of the daily newspaper. Anyway, to improve radio reception, Dad had strung an antenna wire from the turret of our home to the ridgeline of the barn, the wire being perhaps 25 to 30 feet above ground level. Kicking or passing the football was beyond my athletic ability, but Mom could kick that ball right over the antenna wire, and did so again and again. She was really pretty good at this game.

Before bedtime, she washed us in our four-footed cast-iron tub, sometimes two at a time, then placed us on a tub-spanning wooden seat for drying. Once, when I was about five, she noticed me staring at a part of my sister's anatomy which was decidedly different from my own, and from that day onward we were bathed separately! Once I had been tucked in bed, she read stories, which increased in length and vocabulary year by year. An early favorite was *Hooky the Goblin*, followed by Thomas Bailey Aldrich's *Story of a Bad Boy*. With lights out, I tried to sleep, but light seeping in from the hallway revealed dark shapes lurking just outside my room. These creatures, which I named "The Boo Boos," were cause for alarm, and Mom answered my calls by lying beside me until sleep finally came. The Boo Boos haunted me for less than a year, and by the time I entered first grade, they had disappeared forever. By this time, Mom's bedtime readings were more advanced, and eventually included such heroic literature as Virgil's *Aeneas*.

While still a very small boy, I started most mornings by climbing into Mom's bed, where she cuddled me and said, "Now we're twins." Dad got up much earlier because he had diabetes and had to prepare for his self-administered insulin shot, and also had to be at work early to ensure that his Whiting Milk Company drivers started their milk runs on time. Before leaving, he faithfully brought Mom a cup of coffee and some soda crackers. I ate a few of these crackers, but first dipped them in the coffee. Then it was time to get up and start the day hard at play.

Author's dad, Edward A. Hattin, beside Whiting Milk truck at plant on Gannett Road, ca. 1940.

Betty, Marjorie, and Donald Hattin (l. to r.) on our "velocipedes," ca. 1934.

Until I was seven or eight years old, outdoor play was largely confined to riding my tricycle – mom called them "velocipedes," so we called them "velocipedes," – on the driveway or on the floor of our large barn, or to busying myself in the backyard sandbox. One day in 1936, while immersed in sandbox activities, I spied the gas cap of our old Chevrolet, which was standing nearby, and decided to investigate. After removing the cap and peering inside, I cleverly transferred some sand from the sandbox into the fill pipe. Shortly thereafter, Mom drove us to the beach, and on the way back the engine began to miss. Valiantly, Mom nursed the car home, and with some effort coaxed it up our driveway. Dad was more than a little upset, and Mom never drove again.

Our 1928 Chevrolet sedan, 1936.

Mom cooked wonderful meals – always filling and always balanced – and she baked nearly every day. Cakes, cookies, scones, or cupcakes were always on hand, but pie-baking was reserved for Thanksgiving and Christmas, and for Easter Sunday she made hot-cross buns. When making a jelly roll, she'd cut off the edge before adding the filling, and then do the rolling. Once, when my friend Gabriel Jacobucci was visiting, we got to eat all the cut-off crusts. I remember Gabe saying, "Gee, not burned or nothing."[1]

Other than baking, mom excelled at making hard-candy lollipops. These were disc shaped – 2 ½ inches in diameter and 3/8 inch thick – and mounted on round pointy ended sticks. These

---

[1] Gabe was born in Italy and came to the U.S. in time to start first grade. Later, he became an Eagle Scout, a highly skilled mason, and was superb as M.C. of my wife's 30th high school class reunion!

**sticks were inserted into the cooling candy before it hardened.** We all watched with rapt attention, because each would receive one as soon as the lollipops were finished. Vivid in my memory is the time the candy had cooled longer than usual, and while she was forcing a stick into the candy disc, the stick slipped and pierced her hand clear through! She never let out a sound, and I don't remember that she called a doctor.

Each summer, Mom made root beer using Hires Root Beer Extract. This was essentially the only carbonated beverage we had during summer months. She brewed the stuff in a large crock, poured the mixture into one quart gingerale bottles, and applied metal closures with a bottle capper. These bottles were then stacked on their sides, and covered with a cloth until the carbonation process had been completed. Then, very carefully, she straightened up each bottle and took all of them to the cellar for cooling. Very few bottles ever popped their caps. Her root beer was the best I've ever tasted, or so it seems.

Although ice cream was readily available from Dad's milk plant, we often made our own in a hand-cranked, wooden White Mountain churn using ice and rock salt to freeze the cream, sugar, and vanilla mixture. Not one of us ever complained about turning the crank, even when the mixture became quite stiff. Next, Mom withdrew the paddles, which we eagerly licked clean, then packed down ice cream that seemed to outshine any of the commercial brands.

My mom was an excellent seamstress, keeping our sewing machine humming as she made dresses for my sisters and house dresses for herself. For Halloween, she constructed wonderful costumes – pilgrim dresses for the girls on one occasion and really great witch costumes for her three oldest on another.

We were not allowed to use naughty words. During my boyhood, the really bad ones were "hell" and "damn." If such a

Marjorie, Donald, and Betty Hattin (l. to r.) in Halloween costumes made by our mom, ca. 1935.

word slipped out, the perpetrator found his mouth being washed out with Fels Naptha Soap. That soap worked well on clothing and did a most efficacious job on the errant mouth! When I was really naughty, such as being especially mean to my kid brother, she walked quietly but deliberately to a shrub which grew in our orchard. Cutting a long slender switch from the bush, she calmly called me to her side, instructed me to bend over, and applied two or three good licks on my rump or thigh. If my transgressions occurred indoors, she used instead a flat-backed aluminum hairbrush, which was just dandy for occasional spankings. I know now that those punishments hurt her much more than they hurt me.

Mom had a fantastic vocabulary, and did not hesitate to use big words whenever appropriate. However, if when reading I encountered a new word and asked her for a definition, she invariably said, "Look it up on the dictionary." Extensive use of the dictionary became for me a lifelong habit, and all because she had encouraged me to do so.

Mom cautioned us about many things – never play with matches, put nothing smaller than an elbow in your ear, watch for cars when crossing the street, and never ever put puffed wheats up your nostrils. Frankly, I would never have considered putting a grain of puffed wheat up my nostril, but this action was attempted almost as soon as the words left her mouth. Because she feared presence of poisonous gas, she warned sternly against crawling through the culvert beneath a neighbor's driveway entrance. Unable to resist such a challenge, I eventually did crawl through that culvert, but found only pebbles and broken glass.

My mother had a wonderful sense of humor, which manifested itself in many ways, some of which were recitations, some of which were practical jokes, and some of which were naughty. Among the last are these jingles:

> Willie, dressed in the best of sashes,
> Fell in the grate and burned to ashes.
> After a while the room grew chilly,
> But nobody cared to stir up Willie.

Another was:

> Willie drowned his little sister.
> She was gone before we missed her.
> Willie's always up to tricks.
> Ain't he cute, he's only six.

Her practical jokes relied on gadgets she bought at Daddy and Jack's joke store in Boston. Her favorite was a double suction cup, which she used when serving coffee or tea to a guest. When the cup was lifted, the saucer came up with it, causing the guest to gasp and quickly grab hold of the saucer to prevent it from falling and breaking. Another was the dribble glass, which had an etched design near the top that was in places cut clear through. Anyone using this glass soon found the beverage – always water – trickling down his or her chin and neck. Great fun to watch this. Mom also had an artificial ink blot and dark-colored empty ink bottle. The ink blot was shiny, and looked wet. So, with fake ink blot on a white tablecloth and bottle tipped on its side, the effect was quite realistic and fooled everyone who chanced upon it, especially her mother. Yet another of these practical jokes was effected by 5 or 6 card-like pieces of steel, each about 2"x4" in size. After a big meal, such as Thanksgiving dinner with lots of guests, Mom would hold these in her hand while clearing a huge pile of dishes from the table. Once in the kitchen, she'd drop the stack of metal, which hit the floor with the sort of resounding crash made by breaking china. All the guests would jump up and hustle into the kitchen to help clean up the supposed mess, only to find

Mom doubled over with laughter. She really loved playing these practical jokes.

During the late 1930's and early 1940's, Mom occasionally went shopping in Quincy, MA, a small city perhaps 18 or 20 miles distant. Always, she brought each of us some small present – things that were really useful and imaginative. She had mastered the art of keeping us interested and busy. Early on, perhaps in the mid-1930's, the trophies were clay pipes marked "T.D." that were made in Holland. Some were long stemmed, some short, and these were used as bubble pipes. Being fragile, they broke easily, but we usually had a few on hand. Another time she bought me a hammer – my very first "professional" tool! Sometimes it was a small 25¢ can of oil-based paint, at others, a volume of the "Wonder Book" series. These small gifts were in addition to the other items, mostly clothing, in her bulging shopping bag. Her trips to Quincy were not frequent, but she made excellent use of her time there, and we looked forward eagerly to the surprises which were sure to be divulged upon her return.

Mom was always busy, hardly ever just sitting and never taking a nap (unless it was while we were in school). If she wasn't cooking she was washing clothes, mending socks, making beds, canning food, washing the kitchen floor, making clothes, or any of the myriad other chores required of the typical homemaker. Her household equipment was old fashioned, even by standards of the day. An icebox instead of refrigerator; a four-burner gas stove which also had a two-lidded fuel-oil-fired section on which sad irons (she disliked her electric iron) were kept hot throughout the year; and an Easy washing machine that had three concave-down size 48DD cups (just joking) which, with up-and-down plunging action, literally pounded the dirt from our play clothes. Still, she had time to participate in P.T.A., was a member of the Book Committee at Pierce Memorial Library, and was long a member of the Baptist Church sewing circle. She had a strong sense of social justice, and was openly opposed to any form of racial or ethnic prejudice. Despite sewing circle activity, she went to church only on Easter Sunday, but she made certain her four children went to Sunday School on a regular basis.

We were far from being a wealthy family, and Mom engaged in several activities to help with family finances. Being a skilled wordsmith, she created numerous crossword puzzles for *The Boston Globe*, receiving $5.00 for each one submitted. She used real words, never such flimsy artifices as "____ Benny" or "____ Canyon." Looking at her work, I realized how much effort she expended on each, and wondered where she found the time. For several years she was involved in the lunch program at Hatherly School, concocting such treats as fruit cups, hot beverages (cocoa) and soup. Half pints of milk, delivered by the Whiting Milk Company, were part of this program. The cost to participants was very small, perhaps 5 or 10¢ per day. For lunch, I always went home, which was next door.

Alert to all possibilities for added income, Mom saved all of our newspapers and rags, the latter being stored in a large cloth "ragbag" which hung at the top of our cellar stairs. Every few months, Mr. Hymen Cohen, the ragman, arrived in his horse-drawn wagon to collect our accumulated recyclables. Using a hand-held scale, he weighed each bundle of newspapers, for which he probably paid no more than 1¢ per pound. Then, he'd weigh the rags, which brought perhaps two or three cents per pound, and announce the weight to my Mom. Inevitably, he'd place his hand beneath the bag so as to reduce the apparent weight. Just as inevitably, Mom would say, "Mr. Cohen, please remove your hand from beneath the bag." This was a game they reenacted every time "Hymie" came to our house.

When in conversation, Mom usually indicated agreement by saying "ayuh," much as a person from Maine might do. Once, running into the house to ask a question, I found her engaged in telephone conversation with someone who had quite a bit to report. At intervals, Mom would say, "ayuh," and repeated this word many times over a period of several minutes. In fact, except for saying, "Goodbye," it was the *only* word I heard. She was unaware of my presence until she hung up the telephone. Turning to find me waiting patiently she remonstrated, "You've been listening!"

Lastly, Mom wanted to operate a day-care school, although at the time I never heard that term being used. To begin this enterprise she actually purchased crayons, colored construction paper, white paste, and a number of small blunt-ended scissors. Alas, at this time she was already stricken with cancer, which two years later ended her life at the all-too-early age of 49. From the time I was four years old she had made plain that someday I would go to college, and in the fall of 1946, at the age of 17, I entered the University of Massachusetts. Little did I suspect that the most revered of my mentors would pass away before the school year was out.

# Chapter 3
## 612 Country Way

**The House**

During the late twenties, my family lived in an early 19th century house on the corner of Mann Hill and Ann Vinal roads – a Cape which was proving too small for the growing Hattin family. My only recollections of that first home are of sitting on a potty in the middle of the kitchen floor, a partially enclosed dinette-type eating corner, and playing with a green-painted cast-iron race car. In 1931, we relocated to 612 Country Way – the site of a gambrel-roofed, turreted house which had a large porch (we called it "the piazza"), part of which was under roof. A dutch-style front door, the tower, and two beautiful stained-glass windows in the "den" were among the more elegant features of this 10-room cedar-shingled structure. Although Dad had a secure position managing a local milk-distribution plant, these were depression years and we took in a lodger – Mr. Coffin. He took his meals with us, and from my high chair I once declared to him, "You mime you bismus!" My dad was quick to react, saying that I must have learned that from a certain neighboring family! Whether from habit or as a joke, Mr. Coffin put pepper on cantaloupe whenever my mom served that fruit. We tried it and liked it, and to this day I always put pepper on cantaloupe!

Our kitchen was the neighborhood gathering place, and hub of family activities. Mom was always baking cookies and other goodies, which were shared with whoever happened by. The stove was an interesting hybrid device having four gas burners and two oil- burning units, the latter beneath circular, cast-iron lids. An upended 5-gallon glass bottle on a metal stand held the fuel oil, which was fed to the burners through a copper tube.

Our house at corner of Mann Hill and Ann Vinal roads, Egypt, MA, ca. 1930.

Our house at 612 Country Way, North Scituate, MA, 1936. Note turret.

Starting when I was about 12 years old, daily filling of the oil bottle from a 55 gallon drum became one of my regular chores. The oil burners were lit throughout the year, and Mom always kept three cast-iron sad irons heated on the rear part of the stove. Each was marked with a raised numeral – 3,4,6 – for the weight in pounds. My mom spent endless hours pressing clothes for our family of six on her wooden ironing board.

Dinner was served in the kitchen around an ancient drop-leaf table. This was the sole time each day when all of us were assembled in one spot. Meals were delicious because Mom was a great cook. She made do within our means, so we often had meals consisting of cheese soufflé, fried tripe, rabbit, squirrel, or occasionally pheasant. About once a week we'd have steak – a 1"-thick sirloin – or hamburger patties. On Fridays the evening entreé always consisted of fresh fish. All local markets had fresh fish on Fridays to meet the demand of Catholic families, so that was the best day to have fish. All of us loved those fish dinners. Fresh salad was an invariable part of the meal and was served *after* the main course, an olive oil/vinegar/garlic mixture being the usual dressing. A dessert followed, my least favorite being prune whip. We seemed to have it more than any other, and by the time we married, I informed my bride that I would eat anything but prune whip! As dinner was progressing, Dad would turn on our "super heterodyne" radio and tune in the Gabriel Heatter newscast. Some of you will remember him starting off with the phrase, "There's good news tonight." Woe to the family member who spoke out during this nightly ritual, to which my Dad listened with undivided attention.

Following our meal, dishes were carried to a small sinkroom adjacent to the kitchen. Using leftover fragments of hand soap enclosed in a small wire basket, we whipped up suds in the sink water, did the dishes, dried them and put them away. We children had a regular role in this work, and afterward dried our hands on an endless towel which was suspended from a roller on the sinkroom wall. Mother prepared most meals on a table that stood against one wall of that room.

With few exceptions, food was stored in our pantry, which was lined on both sides by shelves packed with foodstuffs, the "good" china, pots and pans, and baking supplies. Bread was stored in a tin breadbox, flour in a small wooden barrel. It as on a dough board in this small room that mom prepared all of the baked goods. Whiskey, a .38-caliber pistol, and ammunition for Dad's rifles and shotguns were kept on one of the top shelves, where some very old tins of pipe tobacco lay moldering away.

The rear of our home comprised a small room we called "the back entry." In it stood our Easy-brand washing machine (described in the previous chapter) and the icebox, into which a 75-pound block of ice was placed by the milkman every four or five days. Drippings from the ice were collected in the "ice-pan," which for several years it was my duty to empty each day. In my early teens, I realized that the back entry was built over earth, i.e., a crawl space. Taking a large wood bit and brace from Dad's toolroom in the barn, I bored a hole under the icebox drain, inserted a funnel, and presto – no more emptying of the icepan. Dad was pretty impressed by my ingenuity, but about a week later suggested that I check the cellar to see if water was leaking into the furnace room. What met my eyes was an astounding 4" of standing water! Of course, I realized at once that two blocks of ice could not possibly have created such a flood, and soon located a pipe which had burst coincidentally with my hole-boring scheme. Ross Schultz, who was a good friend of Dad's, came at once and repaired the damage. Around 1946, we finally did get an electric refrigerator, but by this time my mother was sick with cancer, and had scarcely more than a year to enjoy this new and wonderful worksaver.

Less fortunate was an earlier episode involving an electric cord which had a two-pronged plug at one end and bare wires at the other. Upon plugging this into an outlet, I created a great shower of sparks which was followed by utter darkness throughout the house. Amazingly, our ancient electrical system had but a single circuit and single fuse! Dad got pretty upset about that experiment, and thereafter our house was fitted with *two* electric circuits. Strangely, the entire house contained only two electric outlets – one on the kitchen wall, and one on the living room floor. Necessarily, ceiling light fixtures were used to plug in appliances such as radios, washing machine, and lamps.

Needless to say, we had only one floor lamp, no table lamps, and only two radios. Otherwise, each ceiling light would have had the appearance of an octopus.

Our "den" lay off one corner of the kitchen, and was furnished with a secretary that served as bookcase, writing desk and radio stand. Amongst the books were two written by my great uncle, Harris Hawthorne Wilder (Uncle Hal), and a *Who's Who in America* which contained names of Uncle Hal and two other relatives, all on Mom's side of the family. Also in the den was an iron cot, with trundle bed beneath, that Dad used for his occasional Sunday afternoon naps, and also served to bed down visiting relatives. A set of deer horns and a WWI German Mauser with bayonet adorned walls above the cot. Mom's sewing machine stood against one wall, and a door to the outside, flanked by the lovely stained-glass windows, stood at the far end. My four-wheeled wooden toybox was also in the den, so I spent a lot of time playing in that room, at least until childhood toys were outgrown. Of all my toys only one survives to this day. A Teddy bear with yellow hair, brown eyes, blue and yellow "suit," and felt hand and foot pads was for a time my pride and joy. This wonderful bear entered my life in 1932 or 1933, and became my friend and nearly constant companion for at least three or four years. One day, I decided that Teddy required a haircut. After all, by this time, Mother was cutting *my* hair. So, using the family hair clippers, the kind operated by repeatedly squeezing and releasing the handles, Teddy's curly locks were shorn, and a most raggedy job I made of it. Impressed with my cleverness, I presented Teddy to my mother for inspection. I cried and cried when she told me that the hair would never grow back. As I grew older and gave up childish toys, Teddy was nearly relegated to the scrap heap, because one spring day when snow in the yard was melting, my short-haired bear was found lying on the ground, all soggy, a bit distorted and with rips in his "suit." Once back in the house, he was dried out, got a new set of paw pads, was stitched together where torn, and was thereafter pretty much forgotten. Today, he resides in my mom's old steamer trunk, down in our basement, his hair still not regrown!

One Christmas, my brother received from "Santa Claus" a 16mm motion-picture projector complete with two short black-and-white films, one featuring Charlie Chaplin, the other The Three Stooges. These movies were projected onto a sheet in the den, and we watched them dozens of times until the novelty was totally worn out. Here, too, we watched images projected from Mom's radioptican. Usually, these were postcards or cutouts from the funny papers. For some reason, the machine reversed the pictures such that when we showed a Mutt and Jeff cartoon frame cut from *The Boston Globe*, the exclamation, "Oh boy!" projected as "!YOB HO".

In a corner of our dining room stood a large oak upright piano. This, like the secretary in the den, came from the estate of Great Uncle Hal and his wife, Inez Whipple Wilder, both of whom had lived in Northampton, MA, and had taught at Smith College. Numerous other objects in our home had come from their estate, including such exotic items as a Turkish fez, a Chinese picnic basket, a Turkish puzzle box, and an exquisite white-gold filigreed aquamarine ring which eventually passed to my wife. On the piano, I spent many hours practicing lessons assigned by our neighbor, Cecelia "Cecil" Brown. She charged only 50 cents per lesson – a bargain which was wasted on me because, after learning to play "Animals at the Zoo," I dropped piano (to my lasting regret), and became more interested in other pursuits (see chapter "Construction Projects").

Among all the rooms in our home, the ones I liked best were the turret room, which had windows on 3 of its 8 sides, and the adjoining attic. The former had an electric light and a very old radio of the kind that had a large rectangular box-like base and a separate cathedral-topped speaker. It needed some kind of repair, but I could always manage to tune in one or two stations, however weak the signal. This room had an old brass bed, and at one time was being fixed up for a lodger, but no one ever used it. At about age twelve, I fitted out this room with my chemistry set and made a lot of gunpowder, but never succeeded in causing a decent explosion. From the turret room, I was able to climb out onto the main roof, and from there ascend to the peak of the turret. Then, balancing with two feet on the pinnacle, I was, for an exhilarating few moments, king of the hill!

The adjoining attic was cavernous, and the wide pine floor boards suggested considerable age. It was there that I built a solidly braced workbench on which were mounted a lathe (a Christmas present ca. 1942), a small circular saw, and an equally small drill press. These tools were powered by an induction type of refrigeration motor, which I wired by guesswork (four wires projected from the motor housing) and that was moved to the particular machine I needed. Mostly, I operated the lathe, using it mainly to turn out large numbers of wooden bombs that I painted silver. I also turned out the barrel and cooling jacket of a pretty good replica of the standard U.S. Army .30-caliber water-cooled machine gun. All of these efforts were prompted by WWII. In an old steamer trunk, I found Dad's WWI uniform (complete with roll puttees) and gas mask. Beneath one of our bedroom window seats we found a WWI Springfield rifle. At the time, WWII had erupted, and these items were perfect for acting out the role of a soldier. Soon, however, the government made an urgent plea for these WWI rifles. Many thousands were turned in, including ours, which Dad had brought back from France in 1918.

## A Wondrous Yard

Outside the house, the front part of our property was quite amazing – virtually an arboretum – featuring a wide variety of trees and shrubs, including two giant elms, five maples, a spruce tree, six fruit trees (apple, plum, cherry, pear), a huge lilac bush, butternut tree, smoke bush, quince bush, blackberry bushes, and

Russell Hattin in Dad's WWI outfit, being admired by his older sister, Betty, 1942. Picnic table in background was built by the author

a currant bush. One of the fruit trees, a seckel pear, produced enormous volumes of small deliciously sweet pears each year, most of which ended up being eaten by swarms of bees. Likewise, the apple tree bore much fruit each year, far more than we could consume. We ate most of the plums straight off the tree, and my mother always made use of the cherries and butternuts. In addition to the foregoing, the front yard contained two circular gardens rimmed with hosta, these producing luxuriant blooms each summer. Well, I say blooms, but before most of

The author, standing in front of blackberry bushes which were part of the Hattin "arboretum," July, 1938.

the flowers could open, I squeezed many of the buds between my fingers just to hear them pop. No one ever told me not to!

On a late 'thirties summer's evening our yard was the gathering place for hordes of neighborhood kids, mostly older than me, to play hide and seek, kick the can, or capture the flag. My sisters, both senior to me, were the reason for this congregation, which included "Mooney" and Evie Dorr; Raymond and Elaine Brown; Richard, Robert, Lloyd and Marguerite Fleming; Dominic, Lawrence and Gloria Bonomi; and several others. This group of older kids tolerated my presence, but the more sophisticated games were beyond my capability. Only approaching darkness and mosquitoes brought a temporary end to these frequent festivities. Another favorite game was "giant steps," which was played with smaller, younger groups. Remember this game? A player could advance the number of steps (giant, baby, caterpillar, grasshopper, etc.) only if he/she remembered to say, "May I?"

On a hillslope behind our house, Dad created a huge poultry yard, using standard chicken wire, angle iron posts, and baseboards consisting of lumber collected from North Scituate Beach after a severe northeaster. Within that yard grew a cluster of sizeable slender-trunked gray birches, which I learned very early bent easily without breaking. So, climbing as high as one dared, a kid could launch himself outward, and swing gracefully to the ground before releasing grip on the birch bough. Neighbors and I played in those birches so much that eventually the trunks would no longer spring back to the upright position. That was the end of my birch-swinging days.

My mother spent a fair amount of time on the telephone, often asking the operator to call 149, which connected to Dad's office. One summer day in 1937 or 1938, my brother strolled casually into the house and said to my mother, "149, come down." Puzzled, she asked what he meant, and he repeated, "149, come down." Apparently, he thought 149 was some sort of emergency number. Knowing that Wendell "Ducky" Chipman had come over to play, Mom decided to investigate. Sure enough, there was trouble. While attempting to climb to the top of our overgrown privet hedge, Ducky had slipped, fallen, and got caught *upside down* halfway to the ground. This was just one of Ducky's unfortunate adventures while visiting the Hattin home. Charlie Fleming's luck was not much better!

Using toilet paper and dried corn silk, kids in the neighborhood rolled their own crude cigarettes, which tasted terrible. When dealing with this problem, I remembered the T.D. clay pipes which Mom had bought for each of us to use for blowing bubbles. I figured that with a clay pipe I could have a real smoke. High up on one of our pantry shelves was an old can of dried-out Edgeworth sliced plug tobacco. Snitching a slice, I slipped out behind the barn, crumbled the tobacco, stuffed it in the pipe and lit up. After a few puffs and a lot of coughing, I suddenly felt sick to my stomach, and then got *really* sick! Under normal circumstances, I would have been switched, but Mom knew that the proper punishment had already been exacted. Later, I tried to make cigars by rolling dried maple leaves in brown kraft paper, the result being acrid smoke that tasted and smelled exactly like burning leaves!

Our yard, both front and back, was an endlessly fascinating place to play. One day, while playing cowboys and Indians, I decided to fashion a homemade bow and arrow. With a freshly cut tree branch for a bow I used brown twine as the cord, but the cord was too long, and the excess required removal. Rather than heading to the house to fetch a knife, I decided to dig up and use a piece of glass which I had seen packed in the earth on a path beside our barn. This site was just steps from where the bow was being assembled, and I had trod that path a great many times. Bending down to extract the chunk of glass, I was dumbfounded to see, also packed into the earth on the path, a beautifully shaped arrowhead – my first ever such discovery! Imagine! Until that moment the artifact had remained unnoticed, perhaps for many decades, by all who had previously walked over or stepped on it.

## Our Orchard

Behind our barn lay an orchard of 5 apple trees, including red astrachan, crabapple, a tree bearing fruit which we called "juicy apples," yellow delicious, and one whose fruit was of limited production and unknown heritage. These trees were sprayed three times a year by Mr. John Ford. I remember sitting on a sagging limb of the red astrachan tree, munching on the delicious red-striped fruit. The "juicy apples" ripened late in the season, but the chill fall air did not stop us from sitting comfortably among the branches and eating to our heart's content. When really ripe, the crabbapples made good eating, but most that we gathered were used by Mom for making apple jelly. By the early 1940's, either financial stress or WWII brought an end to the spraying, and the red astrachan tree died. Remaining trees produced good crops right up to the time we sold our property. The old adage, "An apple a day keeps the doctor away," was never more faithfully practiced than in that old apple orchard during summer and fall months.

Our property included 2 grape arbors – one built against the house, another near the back of our property and built over an enormous glacial erratic. The latter supported a dense growth of Concord grape vines, which we never pruned. Nonetheless, each year these vines produced an abundance of sweet juicy fruit which could, by squeezing, be propelled into the mouth. We kids could lie on our backs on the top of the rock, reach up to pluck the grapes, and eat until we were covered with juice. The rock lay near the brow of a hill which descended to the backyard of the Bonomi family. Mr. Joseph Bonomi was a contractor, and once got the job of supplying fill for an expansion of the Whiting Milk Company parking lot on Gannett Road. Mr. Bonomi arranged with my father to excavate that fill from our hillside, the hill being composed largely of loose sand, and to pay Dad 50¢ for each truckload (these were not large trucks). When the digging had been completed, about a hundred truckloads as I recall, the grape-arbor rock was now on the verge of falling downslope. Rather than risk possibility of a fatal accident, it was decided that the rock should be shoved off its precarious perch. Well! After several hours of digging, and use of a huge jack inserted from behind, the rock almost silently slid forward, without tumbling, to the hill's base. Looking on through the whole process, Mrs. Bonomi (Jenny) could no longer see her eldest son, Dominic, and her frantic voice called out, "Where's Dominic." From just below the newly formed cliff edge, came the answer, in a falsetto voice of faked distress, "I'm under the rock!"

## Fun on the Fourth

Fourth of July was one of the grandest of all days, second only to Christmas for unrestrained anticipation. For several days prior to the holiday we watched and waited, and at last Mr. Fabello, our barber, opened his fireworks stand on a patch of ground situated between Henry Turner Bailey Road and tracks of the New York, New Haven, and Hartford Railroad at "The Corners" (North Scituate Village). Clutching coins accumulated over the course of several weeks (or months), in one instance totaling $1.47, I approached the stand in a heightened state of excitement, and reveled in the smell of gunpowder and sight of colorfully wrapped explosives. Few restrictions prevailed, and some really powerful pieces could be purchased and ignited legally. Most potent were the cherry bombs, so named because of their round shape and stemlike fuse, but these were much larger even than bing cherries, and went off with a terrific report. My mother forbad us to purchase these potentially deadly items. Second for noise was the 2" salute, but its sound was but a poor second to that of a cherry bomb. Ordinary firecrackers came in packages of 25, 50 or 100, and could be fired as a unit or unwound and lit singly. It seemed wasteful to shoot off the fun all at once, so I almost always separated these packages and ignited the firecrackers individually. "Zebra" brand firecrackers were loudest of the standard firecrackers, but cost twice as much (something like 20¢ per hundred) as the less effective models. Then there were ladyfingers – tiny firecrackers which were arranged 100 to a row, 5 rows to a package. These were usually shot off 100 at a time, producing a steady popping sound rather than loud bangs. Another favorite was the torpedo – a ball-shaped structure about ¾ inch in diameter – which was set off by throwing it forcefully onto pavement. Torpedoes made a satisfactory racket, but contained something like sand grains which could and did fly outward from the blast so as to sting one's bare legs. Additionally, we bought pinwheels, sparklers, and Roman candles. How I loved the sound and sight of Roman candles! Lastly, we paid a penny or two for some pieces of punk – slow-burning slender wands made of what looked like compressed peat moss – which was used to light fuses. If a firecracker didn't explode, we often would open it and empty the gunpowder onto a board. When the pile was big enough we'd touch it off with a piece of punk and watch with amazement as the powder disappeared in a burst of flame. The first time my brother, Russell, tried this he lowered the punk from above rather than the side, and the resulting flareup burned his hand rather severely. The rest of his Fourth was spent indoors, watching with pain and sadness the considerable fun going on outside. Guess who got blamed?

Our most memorable Fourth of July occurred in 1937 or 1938, when Uncle Irvin Hattin arrived from Connecticut with Aunt Ann, a carload of cousins, and hundreds of fireworks that had remained unsold at his Red and White Store. All of this in a glossy green, long-snouted Cadillac with white sidewall tires that was easily the most elegant car ever owned by any member of the family. Shortly, the grandest of all Hattin fireworks shows commenced, to the delight of eleven family members and assorted close neighbors. Totally awesome, and certainly illegal in Massachusetts, were the 5" salutes – like miniature sticks of dynamite – of which there were a great many. Uncle Irvin lit them, one by one, and hurled them skyward, where they exploded with a deafening blast. The evening show was best – long Roman candles, pinwheels, and large rockets. For firing the latter, Dad and Uncle Irvin nailed two long boards together to form a V-shaped launching trough. The rockets soared skyward, burst into color, and sent a shower of sparks downward. One of the rockets had a mind of its own. Rather than shooting skyward, this particular rocket turned sideways as it left the launching trough and headed across the street, where it exploded just above the heads of onlookers, including George "Pop" Burrill, the principal of Hatherly School. He was not amused.

# Chapter 4
## The Barn

Our property at 612 Country Way boasted a large barn, which was a constant source of fun and amusement throughout the years of my boyhood. That building was a two-part structure, the older and more solid being two-story and gambrel-roofed, and the younger being a two-story lean-to with a roof which sloped so gently that it seemed always to leak. This didn't do that part of the barn much good, and the upper floor became pretty shaky before we sold the place in 1948. The main part of the barn contained a closet (under the staircase), a sliding door at the front, and four multi-light windows. A small alcove housed a large cast-iron press, probably at one time used to flatten documents. Upstairs, this part of the barn contained much old furniture, a corner room with walls which did not reach the ceiling, a large white china thundermug bearing the blue letters "U.S.N.," three large framed prints of a Cunard steamship, a couple of very large hard-covered business ledgers, a lot of black-and-gilt picture frames, some stoneware jugs, and a small doorway which opened to the front of the barn and was overhung by a hoisting beam that had a large eyebolt at its outer end. The rear, lean-to part of the barn had a tool room; a central corridor which housed lawnmower, garden tools, and two old iceboxes; and a large area opposite the tool room which was filled with an assortment of boxes, barrels, chicken wire and other junk, all piled together without order. Upstairs, there was little to see – a three-burner kerosene stove, a rusty iron tire rim, and a small door that opened to the outside were the main features. Well, if all of this couldn't keep a young boy busy, what could?

My earliest memory of a "barn" activity took place when I was 5 years old, just before I started first grade. At that time, my daily playmate was Madeline Riani, whose family lived on a Hollett Street property which adjoined ours. One day, I decided that it would be appropriate to open the small green door upstairs in the back part of the barn, and roll from it the rusty tire rim mentioned previously. Madeline stood below the door, and watched as the heavy rim slammed to the ground not 4 feet from where she stood! Happily for me, and much more happily for her, the rim bounced safely away, thus avoiding potential tragedy. I reported this incident to my mother, not understanding the danger to Madeline and hardly prepared for the severe reprimand that followed.

View of our barn, with author on swing under apple tree, 1933. Glimpse of Hatherly School on left in background.

Russell, with side view of our barn in background, 1933.

Among pieces of antique furniture upstairs in the barn were tables and desks that my sisters, several neighborhood kids, and I used when playing "office." Among the regulars were the Spinzola kids – Lucy, Sammy and Nicholas – who lived on Ann Vinal Road. I remember an occasion when the door handle to the upstairs barn room pulled out, leaving the door locked from the inside. Undaunted, Sammy pulled out his pocket knife, made square the end of a small stick, and while singing the song "ta ra ra boom de ay," fitted the stick into the door latch. To the admiration of all, he then opened the door and gave us a deep theatrical bow. As with most games such as "office," setting up was the most fun, and we really didn't do much regarding the office arrangement once all was in place.

At one end of the second floor, the main part of the barn had a small hay mow and a small quantity of hay. When I was old enough to handle it, I used my dad's scythe to cut tall grass around the back lot, and thus kept a supply of hay up there. The only real use for this hay was for lining nests in the chicken coop, but I liked the idea of using the barn as a barn, and so, just for fun, cut hay for several years. The prospect of a barn fire was so tantalizing that I once swept off a small area within the hay mow and ignited a little pile of hay that I had placed in the clearing. Of course, I immediately stamped out the fire, and later shuddered to think how easily this stupid act of daring could have destroyed the barn and all the neat stuff in it. Until now, I had told only my wife about this incident.

On one occasion, I locked my brother in the small second story barn room, and commenced tossing hay over the wall and onto him. Unbeknownst to me, he was trying to climb the wall in order to escape. Just as I was pitching over another forkful of hay, he let out a yell, and I could tell from the sound that he'd been in the path of the pitchfork. Hurriedly, I dropped the fork to the floor, opened the door and grabbed him. His eyelid had suffered a tiny cut, more likely from a piece of straw than from the very blunt end of a pitchfork tine. Nonetheless, that episode gave me a big scare, netted me a severe scolding from my mother, and made me much more aware of the consequences of youthful pranks.

My favorite "barn game" was hiding from my brother. Many opportunities to do so presented themselves, but the best involved stealthy use of trapdoors. At some point, I noticed that a ceiling area in the back part of the barn was framed by timbers such as to enclose an area about 2 feet square. Puzzled, I went upstairs to inspect the floor above that framed area. The spot was occupied by the old three-burner kerosene stove! Moving the stove away, I spied the two hinges of a trapdoor, and was soon prying this open for perhaps the first time in decades. "Ah," I thought, "this discovery offers great possibilities for the game of hide-and-seek." I called my brother into the barn, and making certain he knew I was upstairs, slipped quietly down through the trapdoor and closed it over my head. He reached the second floor, called me several times, looked everywhere, called again, and finally went downstairs and outside. Quietly, I climbed up through the trapdoor, opened a window, and called him back into the barn. He came speeding back into the barn and up the stairs, hoping to "catch" me, but the old trapdoor trick worked again. I don't recall how many times I pulled this stunt, but eventually I showed him the secret escape hatch. This set the stage for an even more cunning vanishing act. In the left rear area of the main barn, stood a small doorless alcove, which had a ceiling that was substantially lower than the main ceiling. Actually, that little alcove extended back into the lean-to part of the barn, the second floor of which was about 18 inches higher than the alcove ceiling. Obviously, there must be a dead space between the two. With an auger and keyhole saw, I cut loose a couple of the upstairs floorboards so as to gain access to the dead space. Again calling my brother, and making sure he knew I was upstairs in the barn, I lowered myself into the dead space and pulled the loose floor boards into place. He quickly saw that the old kerosene stove was in place, so I couldn't have used the trapdoor. He searched the barn upstairs and down, and when he finally went downstairs, I called out again. He never did find me, but for some unfathomable reason, my dad later discovered where I had cut those floorboards and got really angry at me for what he apparently regarded as an act of vandalism. Why he was upset remained a mystery because we never used that part of the barn for any purpose, whatever.

A final disappearing act involved hammering five large spikes part way into an outside wall of the lean-to part of the barn, above the roof of a small shed I had built there some time before. From atop the shed it was an easy matter to climb to the barn roof using the spikes as hand- and footholds. From a few feet away, these spikes were invisible to all but the most careful scrutiny. The roof was two stories high, and a person lying on the roof could be seen only from the second story of Hatherly School. Russell never could figure out where I was when I vanished before he came around to the point from which I had called. At this time, I was 14 years old.

As recounted earlier, the rear downstairs part of the barn contained a pile of junk that was crying out for order. So, one day I began to straighten up the mess. As the work progressed, there came a most amazing (to me) discovery. Along the outside wall, I found two metal-lined troughs and two vertical two-by-fours, one of which could be moved back and forth sideways. Wow! These were two horse stalls and a cow stall, the last having a device for holding the cow's head while the animal was being milked. Horses for the family carriage and milk for butter and drinking! This explained three raised box-like structures on the floor above that proved to be trapdoors down through which hay could be pitched to the animals below. Of course, I had fun climbing up and down through these openings but never used them to play tricks. Two of the items uncovered during the cleanup were a heavily insulated barrel used for transporting steel canisters of ice cream and a large metal chick incubator which had been heated by numerous clear nipple-ended light bulbs. Our barn was not electrified, but I really wanted to have at least one light so that it would be possible to work there at night. I opened the lid on the old chick incubator and cut out a square of sheet metal containing one of the porcelain light sockets, wired it with a long piece of cheap electrical cord that I had purchased at Seavern's Store, and nailed the socket to a ceiling joist. Then, with a bit brace and large wood bit, bored a hole in the barn wall, threaded the wire through the hole, added a 2-pronged plug, pulled the wire over to our house, and plugged it into an electric outlet. Voila;

an electric light now illuminated the barn. I had purchased a round pedestal-type oak table and four chairs at auction for 40¢, and had visions of building a stage under the light and doing plays, but that project never got off the ground! And was my dad angry when he discovered that I had ruined the ancient (and never-to-be-used) incubator.

The rear part of the barn contained not only the old horse and cow stalls, but also the workshop, which was about 8 feet wide and 12 feet long. All sorts of neat stuff was stored in there, including a block and tackle (the use of which would certainly have annoyed my dad), a workbench with vise, several old blue Edgeworth tobacco tins, a dozen wooden duck decoys, an old carpenters chest filled with a cabinet-maker's tools (including about two dozen wooden planes), an old buggy lamp or two, and assorted hammers, chisels, wrenches, screwdrivers and saws. Despite this plenty, the tools belonged to my father, and were sort of "off limits," although he never actually said so. Therefore, I bought my own tools, eventually assembling a large collection that included bit brace, saws, hammers, try square, shingling hatchet, a plane, and all the other stuff that a kid's tool kit ought to have. My main use of the tool shop was the vise, which I needed frequently. I once bought a vise through the Sears catalog, but the screw broke soon after my purchase, and I never realized the item could have been returned for replacement. At any rate, I did raid the old cabinet-maker's chest in order to use the many planes and chisels that it contained. I remember well that my dad had bought the chest of tools for $5 at auction following the death of our neighbor, Ben Young.

One day, towards the end of my fascination with the barn, I finally got up my courage to use the heavy block and tackle which my dad never touched. Hauling this apparatus upstairs to the front of the barn, I then opened the small green door that was situated above the main entrance. By attaching the double-sheave block to a large eyebolt in the hoisting beam that projected outward above the little door, and rigging a bosn's chair on the single-sheave block, I produced a pretty nifty way of riding up and down by alternately pulling on or releasing (slowly) the one-inch rope. Except for occasionally climbing up the barn roof and walking the ridge line, this was about the last way in which the barn and its features stimulated the imagination of a youth now 15 years of age. By this time, I was thoroughly immersed in scouting activities, and was soon to be smitten by a girl named Margie Macy.

# Chapter 5
## Hatherly School

Shortly after our 1931 move to the big turreted house at 612 Country Way, the decaying wooden picket fence along our north property line was replaced by a new chain-link fence. The workmen also replaced the gate joining our side yard with the adjacent property, which was the playground of Hatherly School. Thus, we had our own access to grounds of the six-grade schoolhouse attended by all four Hattin children. Replacement of that fence is the earliest recollection I have of life at our new location. Later, I discovered that the gate would do me little good during school hours because it opened onto the "girls' side" of the playground, and boys were not permitted to enter any part of the "girls' side," at least not when school was in session.

Before I entered first grade, at the age of five, my two older sisters were already enrolled at Hatherly School. I remember my older sister, Betty, bringing home a *Weekly Reader*, on the front cover of which was pictured the dinosaur *Triceratops*. That picture triggered something in my brain that I am sure

Hatherly School as viewed from our front yard, 1938. Author sitting astride snow horse built after a storm which caused school closure.

led eventually to a career in geology. Each spring, on the 1st of May – May Day – school personnel erected a large wooden pole in the front-yard part of the "boys' side." The pole was festooned with long streamers, which were held by the students – dressed in white – and then wound round the pole as the girls circled first one way, then the other. We also called the

1st of May "Maybasket Day," because on that day we delivered little candy-filled maybaskets to homes of our best friends. My mother made the baskets with cupcake liners around each of which she fastened a band of colored crepe paper. Pipe cleaners served as bails, and each basket was filled with a selection of "penny" candies. We were driven to various homes, where an appropriate number of baskets was deposited on each doorstep. After a knock on the door, we all ran like mad back to the car. If a recipient opened the door quickly enough to catch the giver, the latter person could expect to be kissed. Needless to say, boys gave maybaskets to girls and girls gave maybaskets to boys. I never got caught, thus never got kissed! Sadly, the girls expended little energy trying to catch me. The maypole ceremony and the giving of maybaskets passed into history

Maypole exercise at Hatherly School on May Day, ca. 1933. Note frame of swing set at far left.

as May Day became better known as a national holiday in the Soviet Union.

Jeremiah Ainslie, the bespectacled and mustachioed septuagenarian who operated a small grocery store across the street from the school, once invited me to examine an album of photographs that contained several pictures of the school during its earliest years. Hatherly School was built in 1896 for $8,600, and was originally a stark, square, two-story building with two covered side entrances, one on the "boys' side" and one on the "girls' side." A row of slender maple saplings lined the driveway, which lay perpendicular to Country Way and led straight to the almost windowless front wall. Later, a central, gabled entrance feature was added that included a second story office, and windows were added all along the front walls. With its "schoolhouse-yellow" paint, the edifice had a pleasing aspect that greeted us warmly as we arrived each morning. The school contained six classrooms, and above the front entrance had an "office" remembered mainly because of the dental chair and drill that were permanent fixtures, placed there for semiannual dental inspections and drilling by the school dentist, Dr. Parsons. The office also held certain school supplies, a small stock of athletic equipment, and a stick – the infamous paddle – that our principal, George "Pop" Burrill, used to discipline errant male students. The first floor boasted four classrooms, each with two doors, and each occupying roughly a fifth of the square, first-floor plan. The first- and second-grade classrooms faced Country Way and had a row of windows that looked out onto the front schoolyard. The third- and fourth-grade classrooms lay at the rear, had two walls of windows, and were separated from the other two rooms by a wide hallway which contained two stairways, each facing the other, that led upward in opposite directions to the second-story hallway. Grades five and six were held in two rooms positioned above the third- and fourth-grade rooms, respectively. Each of these four rear rooms had exits to a fire escape that had steel supports, and most surprisingly, wooden steps and landings. The second-story fire escape landing was overtopped by the school bell, a cast-iron affair that was rung by a pull rope. The bell was rung at the start of each school day, after morning recess, and after lunch.

The fire escape was off limits except during occasional fire drills. During these, at the sound of an electric bell, first and second graders filed out the front door, and third through sixth graders exited via the fire escape. From the first floor downward, the fire escape was divided so as to keep kids from the second floor separated from those of the first. Fire drills were fun, and were probably held two or three times a year. We took no time getting coats, because it was "up and out." I do not recollect being cold or getting wet during a fire drill. I may be wrong, but weather conditions seem to have dictated the timing of these drills!

My first-grade teacher was Miss Lucy Lockhart, a tall, dark-haired disciplinarian who taught us by means of a series of flash cards with letters, words and numbers. We had neat orange-covered workbooks containing stories and line drawings that I loved to color by using fat wax crayons. To use a toilet before recess or lunch time, a pupil would ask, "May I go to the basement?" The toilets were located in the basement, which had two parts – one for girls and one for boys.

Hatherly School, ca. 1946. The young lady is Phyllis O'Keefe.

For 5th and 6th graders, this meant climbing down two flights of stairs. The boys' side of the basement always smelled of coal smoke and coal dust because that's where the large furnace and coal bin were located. The janitor, Lewis Newcomb, kept the furnace stoked and did all other custodial duties, including sweeping the floors and staircases. The floors were made of wood – yellow pine most likely – and Lewis used a green-colored, oil-saturated, sawdust-like material to clean up dust or keep dust down. The smell of that oil was ever present in the hallways, and I still wonder just how flammable the oil-soaked wood must have been. I often went to see Lewis after school to watch him shake the furnace grates, shovel ashes into a red wooden wheelbarrow, and push the wheelbarrow to the back edge of the property, where it was dumped. Frequently, Lewis let me sit in the wheelbarrow for a ride back up to the school building, with the seat of my trousers getting pretty dirty in the process. Lewis and I became good friends, and for at least a couple of Christmases I gave him a small present. One year, it was a nail set, another it was a handkerchief. The memory of Lewis and those wheelbarrow rides lingered for more than a quarter century, by which time I was actively seeking just such a wheelbarrow so that I could give rides to another generation of children. Unfortunately, such wheelbarrows had long since ceased to be manufactured so purchasing an old one offered the only prospect. After more than twenty years of looking, and seeing several that were rotted beyond hope of repair, a restorable wheelbarrow was put on the auction block at the Bloomington, IN, National Guard Armory, and I was the lucky purchaser. Twenty five dollars procured the derelict vehicle, which had loose spokes, one original side, one poorly home-made side, a decaying floor and forward wall, and some metal supports which dragged on the floor as I wheeled the squeaking wreck to our car. The basic frame was intact, and just enough of each decayed part remained to enable me to craft exact duplicates. Glue and plastic wood helped restore the largely intact wooden wheel, and three coats of paint produced the desired color. The eventual riders were my grandsons, Whitney and Alan.

But we have strayed from Hatherly School and my first-grade experiences. One of these was vaccination for smallpox, which caused a large scab to form that we were told must not be disturbed. During morning recess we usually played out-of-doors, but on one rainy day, while recess was held indoors, we marched around the room for exercise and I decided to pound each window ledge with a clenched fist while passing by. Miss

Lockhart[1] caught me doing so, grabbed me by the arm, and told me to stop. She inadvertently squeezed my scab and caused a bit of pain, which I reported to my mother that evening. Mom must have contacted Miss Lockhart about this because the next day my teacher was as sweet as pie to me. Most often, recess was held out-of-doors, and in the lowest grades we usually played a game called The King of France. For this, we lined up on one side of the front playground and then, chanting, "The King of France, and forty thousand men, marched up the hill, and then marched down again," we marched back and forth across the lawn. Each day, before school opened, the boys gathered by the side door on the left side of the school, whereas the girls gathered at the opposite side door. Most of the boys had waist-length jackets for use during brisk fall and spring days. All of these jackets had 3- or 4-button closures. On one

---

[1] During a 2005 party at the home of my older daughter, Sandy, I was chatting with an old friend, Don Whitehead, Emeritus Professor of Biology. Don remarked that he had been brought up in Quincy, MA, and our conversation turned eventually to grade school and then to mention of Miss Lucy Lockhart. Don stunned me with the revelation that he had known Miss Lockhart, who was a friend of his mother, and was a frequent visitor in the Whitehead home.

amazing day, however, David Schultz arrived with a new coat that he proceeded to fasten and unfasten with an up and down motion and a "zip/zip," "zip/zip" sound. We were seeing our very first zipper closure device. The year was 1934!

My second-grade teacher was Miss Helen Knox, who was shorter and lighter haired than Miss Lockhart and wore glasses. Second grade was the year for learning subtraction and vying for the privilege of clapping the erasers. This ritual involved carrying blackboard erasers to the side door (the "girls' side" in this case) and clapping them together to clear them of chalk dust. Those who did the best work got to clap the erasers. This was a reward of sorts that was carried out with pride and a considerable sense of importance. According to the Scituate Annual Report for 1936, I had perfect attendance during the 1935/1936 school year! Every year, the entire class was photographed, both individually and as a group. My second-grade class picture is the only one from grade-school days that is in my collection today.

My third grade teacher was Mrs. Sara Souther, who everyone called "old lady Souther." She was probably in her fifties or early sixties, and was easily the oldest teacher I had during public-school years. Third grade was the time for learning multiplication tables and longhand (now called cursive) writing.

*Donald E. Hattin*

Second grade class, Hatherly School, 1936. Class members are identified on reverse side of original photograph, which was furnished by Ward C. "Cobby" Swift. Seated (l. to r.), front row: Madeline Riani,* Jean Mills, Audrey Ainslie;* second row: Thelma Sylvester, Irene Slatro, Olive Dolan, Catherine Anderson; third row: Barbara Forsyth, Priscilla Bonney, Ann Heffernan;* standing, first row: Lindy Harris, Charlie Fleming,* Paul Miles,* Richard Brown, Lawrence Henderson, Cobby Swift,* George Travers, Donald Damon, Louis Cerilli,* Joe Conti, Ralph Roberts;* back row: Jack Litchfield,* Sarge Bartlett,* Donald Hattin,* David Schultz, Nicholas Spinzola. Asterisks indicate those in Scituate High School graduating class of 1946.

*Tales of a New England Boyhood*

Using ruled pages with examples of capital and small letters we drilled every day with ink pens, paper and a smooth movement of the hand that was effected by creating a rolling motion on flesh of the forearm. *Never* were we allowed to bend and twist the hand, which must remain steady while rolling the forearm on its thick pad of flesh.

Our fourth grade teacher was a gem – actually a pearl – Miss Helen Pearl. She had a wonderful, charismatic personality, and commanded the attention of every child in the class while reading aloud to us each day selected stories from a paraphrased bible. These stories emphasized history rather than religion, and were eagerly anticipated by all of us – well, me at least. Fourth grade was the year of long division! How well I remember the exercises – a column of multi-digit numbers that were each to be divided by each of the multi-digit numbers in another column. At this time, hand-held calculators were nearly forty years in the future. Where were they when we really needed them? I do remember Valentine's Day in the fourth grade. We had an exchange every year, but I can remember specifically only that of the fourth grade. Small, inexpensive cards, commonly of the cut-out kind, were given to one's friends, which for some meant every child in the class. If I got 10 or 15 cards, I felt very fortunate. Anyway, it was in the fourth grade that I "fell in love" with my teacher. After school, Miss Pearl graded her papers, prepared the next day's lessons, then walked the mile or so to her home, passing our house while en route. One day, I decided to follow her and find out where she lived. I stayed out of sight as she passed, and then, at the very discreet distance of about 300 feet, I followed all the way to her home on Curtis Street in Egypt. On the way back, I saw classmate Jack Litchfield, who lived in her neighborhood, and told him what I had just done. Somehow, word got back to Miss Pearl, and a couple days later she asked me if I would like to walk *with* her. I was really thrilled, and for the remainder of that school year we often walked together to her home, talking of many interesting things for the entire distance. Undoubtedly, it was Miss Pearl who implanted in me an inspiration for learning that had been less ardent in each of the previous grades. Even so, Mrs. Souther had considered giving me a double promotion, and to this day I am very happy that she did not!

Fifth grade was a still more exciting experience. The old teacher had left, and rumor had it that the new teacher's name was Florence Thelma Annis! My buddies and I were terribly apprehensive, and certainly wary of any teacher whose name was *Florence Thelma*! Well, she turned out to be a sweet, caring and *beautiful* young woman who we (at least I) soon came to idolize. F. Thelma Annis, as she styled her name, smiled a lot, never raised her voice, never spoke a harsh word, and never had to. Several things about that year remain vivid in my memory. One involves the fractions that we now began to study on a daily basis. Another memory concerns our study of U.S. History, and a report I had written and illustrated with drawings to explain how Indians taught the Pilgrims the proper way to plant corn. Miss Annis asked me to reproduce my drawings on the blackboard, and to explain the method to my classmates. I drew several cross-sectional pictures, the first showing a hole in the ground, the next with a few small fish placed at the bottom of the hole, then one with earth on top of the fish, the next with seeds of corn in the hole, then the hole filled and mounded with earth, and the final one with some growing cornstalks. This was the very first time that I lectured to a class, never dreaming that classroom lecturing would one day become my vocation. One of the drollest activities was music class, when the $5^{th}$ and $6^{th}$ graders joined together in one room for choral singing. In order to accommodate the $6^{th}$ graders, we took wide boards from a closet and laid them from one desk seat to the one beside, thus making an extra seat in the aisle. Those, plus the few seats that were always free, created space for the older kids. We sang mostly old favorites, such as "Swanee River,"

"Old Black Joe," and "America," always starting to the tone from Miss Jeanne Bradford's pitch pipe. Art class was another of the more interesting activities, which involved the weekly appearance for one hour of Mrs. Doris Ward. We usually drew Halloween characters at Halloween time, Pilgrims and turkeys before Thanksgiving, and Christmas characters at Christmas time. Almost without exception, Mrs. Ward started the human figure with an egg-shaped outline, which represented the head, and colored it in with pale orange chalk. Dutifully, we followed her example, only with pencil crayons instead of chalk, and on drawing paper instead of the blackboard. Next came the eyes, nostrils, mouth, ears, hat or hair. The body, arms, hands and feet were equally stylized and predictable, but this was a "how to" approach rather than an art-appreciation exercise, and no one seemed to notice the lack of budding Rembrandts in our small class. Doris was the wife of Jim Ward, of whom we shall learn more in chapters concerned with the North Scituate A&P store and lobster fishing. As we neared the end of fifth grade, I became involved with some other class members in building a model of ancient Egypt. This was a *real* work of art, with paper pyramids, the Nile River, and palm trees in an oasis, the water of which was simulated by a small sheet of glass. Walking across the loose desert sand were camels that we cut from construction paper and colored with our brown pencil crayons. As the year came to a close, I spent time after school helping Miss Annis clean up the classroom. I remember wearing white trousers that got *very* dirty during movement of stuff into the storeroom, cleaning up tables, clapping the erasers, and generally making myself useful. I *didn't* want the year to end because I really liked Miss Annis and hated the thought of moving on to the 6$^{th}$ grade. Worse, she had announced that she was *not* returning in the fall.

Happily, the summer of 1939 brought a wonderful opportunity to spend more time with Miss Annis. She was affianced to a young man, Mr. Blakeman, who was a physical education teacher at nearby Pembroke High School. His parents owned a farm in Pembroke that was used by him and his bride-to-be as the site of a summer day camp. I was invited to participate, and believe that a special rate was to be offered if I could round up some recruits. Each day, about 8:00 a.m., Mr. Blakeman and Miss Annis arrived in Scituate to pick up some of the boys, using a huge old boxy Buick of about 1928 vintage – not really so old when one thinks about it. David Schultz and I were two of the Scituate regulars, and en route to Pembroke we stopped to pick up a couple of boys from Marshfield. At the beginning of camp, Mr. Blakeman gave us strength tests at the high school, including lung-capacity tests, strength of hand grip, etc. The idea was that after a couple weeks of day camp, our bodies should have improved in muscle tone and breathing function. At the camp, we did all sorts of fun things, including running foot races and constructing a tree house in the woods well back from the farmhouse. A handyman helped build a rustic cabin, which was the site of indoor activities, including building model airplanes – the sort that were made by use of balsa-wood frames, common pins, paper skin, rubber-band-powered propellers, and what was known as airplane glue. The handyman also built a rooftop frame out of 2x4's for the Buick so that we could carry a boat to various swimming venues. Each afternoon we went to a different pond, all with crystal-clear water, for swimming and fishing. Often, we caught perch and pickerel, but I don't remember that we ate any of these. Mr. Blakeman had a small outboard motor which we used to do some motor boating, and all of us learned to row. One day, while returning from one of the swimming ponds, we passed a motorcycle policeman who was watching for speeders. As we passed, one of the Marshfield boys hollered out, "Hey, flatfoot." About 200 feet beyond the policeman, Mr. Blakeman stopped the big Buick and told the boy to walk back and make an apology. Reluctantly, the boy got out, walked back, and had a fairly lengthy conversation

*Tales of a New England Boyhood*

with the officer. The young man returned to the car in a state of complete humility, said he'd made an apology, and told us how the policeman had accepted his apology, and had then explained the role of police in enforcing the law and protecting the public. All of us learned something from this experience, including the integrity of Mr. Blakeman, the courage required to admit one's mistakes, and the importance of respecting dedicated and understanding peace officers!

On another occasion, a misfortune occurred that I will never forget. While at one of the neat ponds where we were swimming one day, Miss Annis and I began to clown a bit. In water more than waist deep for me, she grabbed one of my feet, lifted it out of the water and lapped the bottom of my big toe! After that, we started tossing back and forth a brick which we had found a few feet from shore. After several tosses, at a distance of about 8 feet, I gave the brick one more toss, just as she averted her eyes momentarily. The brick hit her on the hip, and I could tell by the look in her eyes that she was in a lot of pain, but she never said a word and certainly did not blame me for the mishap. One can imagine the lingering remorse I have felt for having inadvertently injured that precious young woman.

After two weeks of camp, my mother had a talk with Mr. Blakeman and Miss Annis, and it was decided that I would continue day camp for another week. But that week passed all too quickly, and when the old Buick rolled into our driveway for the last time I was heartsick to think my association with Miss Annis was at an end. I rushed to my bedroom, too close to tears to say goodbye. Miss Annis and Mr. Blakeman were married shortly thereafter, and a little later moved to Texas. I never saw them again.

The final figure in this historic sixsome was the principal, Mr. George "Pop" Burrill, who lived in a rented house across Country Way from my home. Pop was an awesome figure, being elderly but not old, wearing thick glasses, appearing a bit stout, and acting with firm authority. Actually, he was a very mild-mannered man, but his lofty position, artificially stern demeanor, and freedom to use a paddle on recalcitrants led us to believe otherwise. Pop was not only principal of the school and $6^{th}$ grade teacher, but also director of the athletic program for older boys. These activities took place during morning recess and during lunch hour. One of our favorite (and much-played) games was ring toss. The court was in a rear corner of the schoolyard (boys' side, of course), and was fitted with two tall posts which supported a rope that extended from one to the other perhaps 7 or 8 feet above the ground. Pop included, we would fling a rubber ring – actually a miniature automobile tire about 6-7" in diameter – back and forth, hoping the opposing team would miss a catch. This resulted in a score for the throwing side. At a signal, Pop would send one of us scurrying to ring the bell that summoned all back to the classrooms. I always tried to stand as close as possible to Pop, hoping he would take notice and send *me* to ring the bell! The other game that we played was a form of baseball known as "scrub." When lunch had ended, Pop would hand one of the boys, usually Johnny Crane, a baseball bat. Johnny would burst forth from the basement door and holler, "scrub," another kid would holler, "scrub one," another would yell, "scrub 2," and so on until a batting order had been established. As I recall, scrub was the batter, scrub one was the catcher, scrub two was the pitcher, scrub three the 1st baseman and so on. There were lots of outfielders. Scrub had to hit the pitched ball and run to first base and back. If tagged out, he took last position in the outfield, and everyone moved up one place – catcher to bat, pitcher to catching position, and so on. This was great fun, but getting clear title to the batting order required a little ingenuity, so I never tried to call scrub, scrub one or scrub two. I waited until I heard, "scrub two," and instantly hollered, "scrub three." This was the position I usually captured. At the end of lunchtime play period, Pop would once again send one of the expectant boys up the fire escape to ring the bell. Everyone loved to ring the bell, and some of us got to do it often. Sometimes after school, even after dinner, we'd sneak up the fire escape and reach up with a pole to ring the bell. Other times, we'd just peg stones at it to make it ring. Climbing on the fire escape after school or any other time was strictly prohibited, so as a pre-teen I felt very daring about ringing that bell without getting caught, and never did.

All through grade school, but especially from third grade onward, we played games with marbles. The boys made a small cup-like hole with the heel of one shoe, turning round and round until the hole was dug and then patting the rim to make it smooth. From an arbitrary distance, we tossed marbles toward the hole. The boy whose marble came closest or even rolled in went "first," and with his index finger curled, knuckles downward, would hit as many of the marbles into the hole as possible. When he missed, the boy who threw next closest took over, and continued until *he* missed. Then the third closest would take over. Whoever hit the last marble into the hole got to keep all of them. Sometimes, each of us tossed two, three, or more marbles, making the "pot" even more attractive. Before play began, we agreed that there would or would not be "clearsies." This meant brushing debris from the path between marble and hole. "Dragsies," or dragging the finger along the ground while hitting a marble, was prohibited. If caught doing "dragsies," the violator ended his turn. Most of the marbles were milky white, with swirls of one or more bright colors mixed in, or were clear glass with swirls of color mixed in. Some marbles were just clear glass, these going by the name "glassies." Every now and then, a boy would bring a few of the older style clay marbles to school, and we had to decide whether or not we would allow "claysies." Usually, we did not.

After school, when anyone could venture onto the "girls' side" of the school grounds, we boys would hoot and holler when viewing the marble holes used by the girls. "Pits" would be a better term because some were nearly as large as a half-bushel basket. Several of these large holes lay along the foundation wall. Apparently, the girls stood back a few feet and tossed a certain number of marbles into these pits, the person tossing in the greater number winning all. It's a wonder they ever missed! My future wife, Margie Macy, became so covetous of her marble collection that her mother took the marbles and hid them from sight. [2]

---

[2] Many years later, long after we married, Marge retrieved the collection and has it today – still in the original Fannie Farmer chocolates box from about 1940!

On the north side of Hatherly School stood a pair of swing sets made of sturdy steel pipes, but all we ever saw were the large steel frames. The swings had been removed years earlier because, we were told, someone had been hurt by falling off or getting hit in the head. It's a wonder the Board of Selectmen didn't outlaw the use of cars in our town. Surely people got hurt by them from time to time, but people continued to drive just the same! Anyway, one of the swing frames had a horizontal chinning bar that we boys used (after school, of course) for doing "pinwheels." We'd climb up to the bar, then straddle it. With a loose encircling grasp on the bar, we would then pivot our bodies round and round the bar – more in the fashion of a propellor blade than a pinwheel. When I got to be of high-school age, I often shinnied up one of the slanting corner supports and hunched out onto the horizontal crossbar from which the swings had once hung. This bar, actually a steel pipe about four inches in diameter, could not be completely encircled by the hands, but I could still do pinwheels up there and often did, mostly when there was no one around to "tell" on me.

The front yard of Hatherly School was divided by a tree-lined drive that led to the front door. On the boys' side the front yard was flat, but the girls' side had a short steep hill that adjoined the Hattin property. In winter, this was our favorite sledding place. Often, many of the neighborhood kids gathered there after school on a snowy day, and we Hattins joined them via our "own" gate to the school yard. Someone always built a "jump" in mid-slope, which we negotiated with sleds, skis, and occasionally a lengthy toboggan. Flexible Flyer sleds were considered to be supreme by those best qualified to judge.[3] The skis were another matter. These were simple oak (or maybe it was ash) affairs, drilled through horizontally about mid-length, and fitted with a single leather strap that one buckled across the instep. Just as soon as snow got between skis and shoes, the skis slipped sideways with disastrous results. Little wonder that we didn't do much skiing until much later in life, starting around age 60. Once in a while, about every third winter, we'd get a snow and ice condition across the entire school property, and could then sled all the way from "our" gate to the lower end of the school grounds, which included an enclosed depression. In springtime, when the snow melted or we had a really heavy rainstorm, the depression filled with water to a depth of 3 to 5 feet in the center. Many times, I'd pull on my rubber hip boots and wade out as far as was safely possible in this small pond,

---

[3] As with the marbles, Marge still has her 1930's Flexible Flyer, complete with eagle emblem and sled in great running condition.

but now and again the water froze and we could do some skating. However, the pond was a very temporary feature, the water accumulating with amazing rapidity and disappearing almost as quickly as it had appeared.

One final memory of Hatherly School concerns the celebration of Christmas. In addition to cutting out paper candles and trees and pasting them on classroom windows, we all gathered in the hallways to sing Christmas carols on the last day of classes before the holiday break. Students from the upstairs classrooms arranged themselves on the two staircases, facing each other, whereas kids from the downstairs classes occupied the main hallway. Then, at the sound of a pitchpipe, we sang all the old-time carols, and ended the fall season with feelings of joy. Christmas was just a few days away!

I truly loved going to Hatherly School, and have a profound respect for the dedicated teachers who helped us to embark on our lifelong journeys of learning.

# Chapter 6
## North Scituate Beach And Beyond

At the ocean terminus of Gannett Road, a break in the seawall known as "first gate" led to the fine stretch of beach where as children and teenagers we spent many a happy hour playing in the sand or frolicking in sparkling Atlantic waters. Severe storms have long since washed away much of the sand, leaving behind a mantle of pebbles and cobbles, which in places along the seawall now lie beneath several feet of water at high tide. How different this beach was during my boyhood! Then, a refuge from advancing waves could be found during all but the most extreme of high tides (full moon, onshore wind), and at ebbtide water's edge lay scores of feet from the seawall. I recall with affection the sort of day my family spent on North Scituate Beach, where my mother, and later my father, took us nearly every pleasant day all through the 1930's. Initially, our transport was a box-like disc-wheeled 1928 Chevrolet sedan that Mom parked in the 8-car lot adjacent to "first gate." In that lot, cars were arranged four abreast in two rows, cars of the inner row being blocked from leaving by cars of the outer row. In reality, inner-row cars were not trapped, because owners of outer-row cars left keys in the ignition so that those vehicles could be moved by whoever wished to exit the inner row. Motorcycle policemen patrolled the area, seeking cars which did not display a Scituate beach sticker. One of these was a solidly built, rather stern-looking officer named "Tickey" Stanley. Where he got the name "Tickey" is uncertain, but I always assumed it was because his idling motorcycle engine created a quiet ticking sound.[1]

From the parked car we lugged assorted paraphernalia through "first gate," proceeded to our favorite spot a few yards to the left, and began the ritual of "setting up." Mom erected our large green-and-orange umbrella, and instructed us to find some small rocks for bracing the wooden pole. Next, she spread out a blanket and called for more rocks so that we could anchor the corners. Soon, we scampered to the water's edge where, under Mom's watchful eye, we'd get wet, splash around in the

---

[1] In 1999, I attended a neighborhood dinner dance in Silverthorne, Summit County, CO, that had been arranged by my daughter-in-law, Vicki. One of the attendees was a young man named Fred Stanley, whom I had been told was from Scituate. He is "Tickey" Stanley's grandson!

water, and dig holes in the soft sand. Of course, these holes always filled with water and the sides caved in, so our efforts to "dig to China" were invariably unsuccessful. Mom was careful to corral us under the umbrella from time to time, and thus prevent nasty sunburns – at least most of the time. Mother always brought along an insulated green one-gallon water jug, some soda crackers, and a jar of homemade jelly. At mid-afternoon, she rounded us up, spread the jelly on several crackers, and offered some also to any friends who happened by. On one occasion this included Matthew Miles, who accidentally dropped his jelly-covered cracker on the sand. Dashing into the water, he rinsed off the sand, ate the cracker and pronounced it delicious. Thus tempted, we all ran into the water and dunked our crackers. Frankly, the result was more soggy than tasty, and the novelty wore off in a single afternoon! Another favored snack was ice cream, which we purchased from the "Good Humor" man. His daily arrival was announced by jingling of bells, which brought us flocking to the truck as surely as if he was the Pied Piper of Hamlin. Usually, we bought "Hoodsies" – ice cream in a small, lidded paper cup that was eaten with a flat wooden spoon. Another favorite, coming into existence later, was the so-called "Pushup," which comprised an ice-cream-filled cardboard cylinder from which the frosty confection was

Mom and her children on North Scituate Beach, 1936. Left to right: Marjorie, Russell, Mom, Donald, Betty.

extruded at one end by means of a plunger pushed in from the opposite end. These cost 10¢ each.

When I was about seven years old, Mom took us to the beach for morning swimming lessons, which I believe were conducted by the Red Cross. First, standing about waist deep, each of us was taught to hold his/her breath and immerse our faces in the water, with waves passing every few seconds. Water temperatures ranged between 63° and 77° F, and during my first lesson were at the low end! Lesson one mastered, we were next shown how to wrap arms around our knees and perform the "jelly-fish float." Next came the prone position, face down, arms extended, in the so-called "dead man's float." Then came the serious stuff, with a stroke known universally as the "dog paddle." The breast stroke and side stroke came next, by which time complete confidence had been attained. I could swim! During the mid-1930's, the town anchored, a few dozen feet offshore, a large (8 or 10 feet square) well-built raft buoyed by 55-gallon steel drums. At high tide that raft was in water way over my head, but at low tide dives had to be rather shallow. When the raft was first put in place, I was still pretty much a dog paddler, but Mom never seemed to worry about my safety. The raft was a tremendous asset to swimmers and divers, being a fixture off "first gate" for two or possibly three summers. Then, for reasons never made clear, the raft disappeared, and was ever after sorely missed, at least by me.

Along the seawall between first and second gates were four concrete staircases known appropriately as "first steps," "second steps," and so on. During the past 75 years, the seawall and steps have been severely storm-damaged and repaired several times. Unfortunately, the raging northeast storms have removed much of the beach sand I knew as a boy, and a couple of features have not been replaced. In the "old days," a freshwater shower was in place at "second steps," and it was there that we could wash off salt before drying ourselves with towels and heading home. Best of all, on a signboard at "second steps," the water temperature was posted daily. Certainly, this was unnecessary

Betty, Marjorie, and Donald Hattin at "first steps," North Scituate Beach, ca.1933.

because all of us went into the water regardless of the temperature, but we always ran to check anyway.

As small children, we acquired the familiar assortment of beach toys – tin pails, tin sand sifter, sturdy steel shovels, and an assortment of rubber balls – nothing, of course, to compare with technologically advanced toys of modern times, but at least ours weren't made of plastic, and they were made in the U.S.A. We built our share of forts, pirate ships, and cars; dug our quota of holes; made many "drip" castles; and enjoyed burying each other – all but heads of course! Amongst our most favored constructions was a large conical mound whereon we molded a spiral chute, which passed through the mound about halfway down. A tennis-sized rubber ball worked best, and when started at the top, rolled down the chute, passed through the tunnel, and continued onward towards water's edge as far as we cared to mold the chute. Another favorite was a race car in which the cockpit featured seat, gas, and brake pedals made with flat pebbles, and a steering wheel made from bits of driftwood. Construction of anything was the important part of sand sculpting, because once the thing was built we seldom played with or in it for more than a few minutes. Another activity involved the "hips" that were (still are) produced in abundance by the beach roses growing in clumps at several places between the seawall and street. These solid fruits make excellent ammunition, so we often pegged them at each other, fortunately without ever doing bodily harm. Often, when the wind was blowing offshore, we'd see a beachball heading out to sea. These balls were nearly always gone for good because they moved rapidly, and an offshore wind produced water far too cold for a major swim. In one instance, however, when our beachball got away and headed offshore, Jimmy Travers, who was a couple years older than me, actually swam far out to retrieve the ball and kindly returned it to us when he reached shore.

The chilly waters accompanying offshore winds are clear and blue, contrasting markedly with the warm choppy green water which accompanies an east wind. The latter condition favored swimmers, but there was a tradeoff. East winds carried shoreward all sorts of debris and junk, ranging from seaweed to Boston sewage, which in those days was poured into Massachusetts Bay almost untreated and was all too easy to identify. (Ugh!) At various times, some really neat stuff washed in on east winds. On one occasion we came across a large ocean sunfish, on another a large seal, and we often found ourselves swimming amongst large red jellyfish which could and did inflict an irritating sting.

During the 1930's, it was not uncommon to see large sailing vessels passing by far offshore. These, we were told, were lumber schooners coming down from Maine and heading for the Cape Cod Canal or making the return trip northward. Some evenings, Dad drove the family down to the parking lot at "first gate" so that we could watch the brilliantly illuminated "New York boat," a passenger vessel, pass by en route to the canal and the big city. Until the late 1930's, some senior class outings involved a trip to New York City on that ship, but the onset of WWII apparently ended such exotic celebrations.

As I grew older, to ten or eleven years of age, my friends and I discovered diving sites around the landmark known as Well Rock, which is a glacially sculpted mass of granodiorite (not a term we used in the 'thirties) that is cut by large, dark colored dikes (we didn't know that term, either). Erosion of the larger dike produced a shaft resembling a well, hence the name. During Victorian times, a wooden stairway and summit platform graced the rock, but by the 'thirties their former presence was betrayed only by rusted iron fastenings (still there in 2005). At low tide, it was possible to enter a narrow cave-like opening on the seaward side of Well Rock and crawl to a point where, by climbing upward, one could emerge at the summit via the so-called well. I made this transit several times, and suspect that few others have done so. Getting stuck in the passage during an incoming tide would put severe limitations on chances for survival!

Well Rock, Minot, MA.

We kids spent a lot of time around Well Rock, mostly in the late 1930's and early to mid-1940's, when travel to the beach was nearly always by bicycle. Little need to lock up our bikes in those days. We parked them at "first gate" with no worry of possible theft, because it just didn't happen. Well, it did happen once, but to my older sister, Betty, whose beautiful blue Columbia-brand bicycle was stolen, stripped of useful parts, and dumped into a Scituate Harbor estuary. The youthful culprit was caught, and made to pay for needed restoration!

About 200 yards offshore from "second gate," and joined to land by a stony tombolo, or "bar," lies Bar Rock, which can be reached at low tide by walking on barnacle encrusted cobbles, or at high tide by swimming.[2] The rock itself, like Well Rock, comprises a low, rounded mass of pale grayish orange granodiorite that was sculpted by a passing glacier and marked

---

[2] During the 1980's, four of us, all in our late fifties or early sixties, commenced swimming to Bar Rock at high tide. On his surf board, a no-nonsense lifeguard overtook us, warned us of the danger (what danger?), and asked if we could touch bottom. We were "way over our heads," but in a pretense of extending my leg downward, I reported that the bottom could indeed be touched. Satisfied that these old fogies were not in trouble, he paddled back to shore, and we continued our swim to Bar Rock. Even as youths, did any of you do that?

with grooves cut by moving ice. Bar Rock is a dandy place to examine animals inhabiting tidal pools, or view salt deposits formed by evaporation of seawater from shallow depressions high on the rock.

In those days – early 1930's to mid-1940's – there was no sunblock, at least none that we knew of, so sunburn was inevitable, especially in early summer before a healthy tan had been acquired. With skin turned bright red, and suffering considerable pain to boot, one had no choice but endure the consequences of overexposure. I remember lying on my belly in bed at night while my mom smeared a mixture of baking soda and water onto my severely burned back. This cool mixture soothed temporarily, but when dry the resulting crusty coating cracked and tugged at the skin with each movement, causing additional discomfort. After several days, the pain subsided and the damaged skin began to peel, sometimes in several-square-inch sheets. In hindsight, this was a ghastly condition made even less enjoyable by the younger of my two sisters, who practically begged me to let her separate the skin from my body.

At the north end of Minot lies a hilly juniper-covered tract known as "The Glades," which is bordered on its seaward edge by large expanses of grayish orange-colored granodiorite. Lying adjacent to the Glades entrance are two rounded masses of rock that are separated by a crevice through which, at proper tide levels, wave-driven water surges so as to form a natural sluiceway. With several friends – girls and boys in their earliest teens – I spent many hours being sloshed along in this chute, oblivious to the bumps and bruises created by the not altogether smooth surfaces. Before WWII, I was too young to venture beyond the Glades entrance, and during that war the area was off limits because of military fortifications. First, a concrete observation tower was constructed on the property, and later a much taller observation tower was built. After the war, when military presence was withdrawn, some friends and I discovered remains of an anti-aircraft gun emplacement, complete with concrete pads for the gun mounts and a surrounding barricade of sandbags. Danger from German submarines was real and ever present, with planes and blimps constantly patrolling the coastline. Flotsam; in the form of life jackets, packing crates, bunker oil, and other debris littering our beaches through much of the war; was clear evidence of Allied ships being sunk just offshore, and many were! Indeed, fighter aircraft occasionally strafed Bar Rock, dropping .50-caliber shell casings which we found washed up on the beach. On one occasion, in mid-winter during wartime, an airplane strafed what was thought to be a German submarine, but was actually a 65-foot-long Right whale. This monstrous mammal washed ashore in Cohasset, and despite very cold weather began to emit the nauseous odor of decay. To get rid of the beast, town officials suggested that whale meat might serve as fertilizer for privately planted victory gardens. Gullible folks lugged great chunks of smelly flesh to their homes, discovering too late that this was just a scheme to clear the beach. Eventually, a Coast Guard vessel towed the carcass out to sea and set it adrift. If any U-boats were sunk or captured off our shore, such news was suppressed by wartime censors.

# Chapter 7
## Construction Projects

Ever since my early boyhood, the prospect of building things has held considerable fascination. Almost as soon as I could hold one, my mother bought me a hammer, and my father gave me small supplies of nails from his workshop. These nails were of assorted sizes and were always handed to me in one of the small cardboard boxes in which pea seeds were then sold. My earliest project, at about age eight, was to pound a series of 8-penny nails into one of our front-yard maple trees to serve as steps for climbing to the lowest branches. Of course, those nails bent downward under my weight, but the problem was solved by simply driving in one or two more nails at each "step."

The first major construction project involved building a train. Together with my sister, Marjorie, we created a steam locomotive and a passenger car using available crates and old boards. The engine boiler was a heavily insulated parallel-sided barrel of the sort once used to ship large steel cans of ice cream. This was supported by a packing crate. A tin can served as the smokestack, and we placed wheels against the sides. The train was stationary, of course. The "passengers" were neighborhood friends, who were given "money" made of sheet lead which had been cut into crude squares by means of tin snips, and was collected by the conductor. Our passengers quickly discovered a way to get twice as many rides. With hands behind their backs, they grinned cunningly, bending each lead square to and fro until it broke into two "coins." I remember clearly that Charlie Fleming, who later became a four-year president of my high-school class, and who for reasons then and still unknown is called "Pete," was one of the culprits! Some of the wood for our train came from our barn floor when builder Chester Spear did a repair job, and the lead was old flashing which came from a roof area of our house that he repaired at the same time.

Once revealed, our skill at building things knew no bounds, and we began to gather materials to build a playhouse. When the Whiting Milk plant on Gannett Road was repaired around 1939, a number of 2'x12' planks became available for our use, and partially rotted sill supports from the barn repair job became pilings. Some of the milk-plant 2x12's were used for sills. We laid them flat-wise and notched the corners for a neat fit. Studs were erected at each corner and at the door position. Siding was applied, leaving a 2-foot-wide door opening, and on either side of the door and on each end of the hut, we left openings for windows. Picture frames discovered upstairs in the barn were nailed into place to form window frames. These were gilded-and-black frames which today would be considered valuable antiques. We ruined them with 8-penny nails! Our dad took measurements to Ray Litchfield, a friend and proprietor of a garage in the West End, and Ray cut auto window glass to fit the frames. Narrow boards were used to hold the glass in place. The door was fitted with hinges, and opened outward. When construction reached ceiling level, we began to add a steeply pitched roof. At each end of the hut we erected a vertical plank, which we notched to receive a ridgepole. We had a neat two-seat swing set, which our dad had suspended from a 10-foot length of 3"x4" fir that spanned the distance between two cedar support posts. I climbed each pole in turn and cut out the main length of 3x4. This became the ridgepole, and I remember my Dad getting pretty angry about me having ruined the swing set. No matter, because we didn't use it anymore. After the ridgepole was in place we erected rafters, three on each side, added roofing boards, and boarded up the gable ends. We made a hole in the ceiling and added a hinged trap door, which was opened from below by means of a rope and pulley system. Then came the crowning touch. Dad bought us a square of cedar shingles – about $1.40 in those days – and a roll of tarpaper. The latter was applied to the roof, one strip on each side and a third strip wrapped across the ridge. We used proper tarpaper nails and tarred the joints before applying the third strip. The shingles were just sufficient to cover the front of the hut, and we made a proper job of it after having watched Mr. Spear re-shingling part of our house. We planted hollyhocks on either side of the door, and for good measure painted a large orange dot on each shingle. Fortunately, our mom photographed the hut, a picture of which is included here. Total dimensions of the hut were approximately 8 feet wide 4 ½ feet deep, and 7 to 8 feet tall. We played in the hut regularly for about a year or so; however, as was usually the case, building it was the greatest fun.

Russell (left) and the author in front of "hut" built by Donald and Marjorie Hattin in 1939.

A year after we built the hut, further construction at the Whiting Milk plant resulted in a large supply of flooring boards from a re-built ice chest. This was used to construct a second room in the form of a lean-to at the back of our original building. By this time, I was eleven years old, and did the addition by myself. An original wall was breached to connect the two rooms, and a single never-to-be paned window admitted light. The roof was tarpapered, but the sides were never shingled. Again, construction was the real fun, and we really didn't play in it very much. I do remember placing a potbellied cast-iron stove in the second room, but it was never lit.

At about the same time, 1939 or 1940, we built what passed for a large sailing ship. First, we laid several of the discarded milk-plant 2x12's side-by-side to form the forward deck, and an equal number was used to form the after deck. Two posts were laid down to form the prow, and a stout pole was erected amidships to serve as the mast. Guy ropes tied to stakes held the pole firmly upright, and spikes driven into the mast served as steps up to a cross arm, which also served as crow's nest. The pilot house was a box, and a spare board became the gangplank. Logs were used for cannon, and a rock fastened to a rope was our anchor. Not much to look at, perhaps, but that ship carried us on several imaginary voyages. As with most things we built, the fun was primarily in the construction process, so we soon tired of the ship and cast about for a new project.

At about this time, my brother was pretty thick with Wendell "Ducky" Chipman, who lived a short distance down Country Way towards North Scituate Village, and one day Russell told me they had made a tree house. Naturally, I wanted to see this, and was appalled by their poor workmanship. Basically, they had nailed an old door between some branches of a large cherry tree at a height of about 8 feet off the ground, and this door sloped crazily at an angle no less than 20 degrees. Surely, something better could be built, so we rounded up some old 2x4's, some 1"-thick boards, some nails and a saw. I brought my hammer from home. First, I spiked two 2x4's across the lower branches, these members being nearly parallel to one another and at approximately the same distance off the level ground. Next, I built a floor by nailing several 1"-thick boards to the 2x4 "joists." Then, I nailed a series of short boards crosswise onto the tree trunk to serve as a ladder. All of this took perhaps 3 hours. The younger boys were elated at the improvement, but much more was possible. Why not add a second story to the treehouse? By nailing more cleats to one of the thicker branches, I could climb to about 16 feet above the ground, and there spiked a couple more 2x4's to the largest branches, and built another deck. At this altitude, the branches were only about 3" thick, so the second platform swayed a bit, but no matter – it was usable.

Standing nearby was another large cherry tree, which also had a number of thick branches. It struck me that by building a platform high in that tree, we could construct a bridge from one tree to the other. So, I nailed cleats up the main trunk and thickest branch, hauled up two 2x4's and spiked them into place, and added deck boards. Next, we hauled 2 long 2x4's up to the new platform, and jockeyed them into position 18" apart so as to span the distance between the two high platforms. Nailing boards crosswise along these rails completed the bridge. During bridge construction, I lost grip on my hammer, which fell and hit Ducky on the head. Fortunately, the hammer fell at an angle so that the handle hit only a glancing blow, and after a few harsh words from Ducky, we all got back to work. The bridge had no handrail, and swayed dangerously when in use. Again, the fun was in the construction, and I never played in that Rube Goldberg edifice.

My attention turned next to the possibility of raising chickens, as my father had some years before. The old chicken house was large (about 12x24 feet) and ugly, and the grain had attracted rats, so he asked me to tear it down. To raise chickens, therefore, I would need to erect a new, smaller, more efficient coop. The studs came from the old chicken coop, a few of the siding boards were donated by our neighbor, Mrs. Ben Young, and the rest of the building materials as well as roofing and siding paper, came from the Welch Company – at my expense, of course. The sills were laid on rocks and chunks of concrete so as to level the floor on what was a relatively steep slope. A hole in one wall served as entrance for the chickens, and a shed-type roof was pitched to drain rainwater. Sills, flooring, studs and plates were installed in a fashion which would meet such building codes as may have existed at the time. I had learned the techniques by watching carpenters at work, and from having made mistakes building the hut. The door was hinged, and fastened with a hasp and wooden pin. From Mr. Fred Litchfield, Ray's father, I purchased a dozen Rhode Island Red pullets and a sack of grain. When the hens started laying, I sold eggs at 50¢ per dozen to my family and to Mr. and Mrs. Job Vinal, who lived atop a lane across the street. Once a month, Mr. Ronnie Melman, who worked at the Welch Company, furnished a burlap sack full of wood shavings for the coop floor, and for this service received a dozen eggs. Soon, I learned that all of the potential profit was being consumed by purchases of grain at $3.00 per hundred pounds and by trading for wood shavings.

Also, the chickens got infected with lice, and one got cropbound and had to be held by its feet while we squeezed its throat to empty the crop. Each hen that stopped laying was purchased by my mom for 50¢, and ended on the dinner table. All too soon, I was out of the egg business, forever!

About this time, my reputation as a builder was growing, and when Mr. and Mrs. Harry Chipman learned of my chicken coop, they commissioned me to build one for them. Oddly enough, no mention was made of building materials, although some scraps of lumber were piled behind the Chipman's garage, and there were plenty of nails in paper bags in that garage. However, I scrounged most of the boards for siding, roof, and door from neighbors, the majority coming from my friend and Hatherly School janitor, Lewis Newcomb. Those came from some sort of mill or shed on his property that had been torn down years earlier, and had been stored under canvas. In a week or less, the 7'x7' chicken coop was completed, and Mrs. Chipman invited me into their home for payment. At the time, she was not well, so we met in her bedroom, where she thanked me and gave me $2.00 – a handsome sum at the time (1940). Apparently, thinking that $2.00 was not enough for all my work, she also handed me a new toothbrush. After all, I had furnished all the labor and at least three-fourths of the lumber! Anyway, I was delighted because the coop had been a challenge and there was great satisfaction in completing the job. The Chipman's never used the coop for chickens – it became a playhouse for Ducky and his friends, Joe Santia and Marsh Litchfield.

Next in the series of construction projects was an underground hideout, which was dug near the rearmost boundary of our acre-plus property. The quickest way to accomplish this was to dig a deep trench, roof it with timber, and cover the timbers with earth and sod. Much to my surprise, we could dig down only three feet before hitting a strangely tough layer of clay – hardpan formed presumably by the enormous weight of Pleistocene glacial ice. Of course, we did not understand the origin of that hardpan. We started digging near the southern edge of our property, which was the steep side of a sandpit, and dug a ditch 3 feet deep and 3 feet wide. All kinds of scrap timber and boards were used to create the roof, and at the midpoint we dug a circular room about 5 feet in diameter. Beyond that, the passage ended blindly, but I cut and cased a 2-foot by 2-foot opening in the ceiling and fastened to the accompanying trap door enough sods to make this door invisible from the outside. One of our first activities in this hideout was also one of the last. While a neighbor boy was in the circular room, we built a fire at the main entrance. He tried to escape through the trap door, but a couple of the kids stood on it to prevent escape. After two or three minutes, we realized he was coughing loudly, so we opened the trap door and hauled him out. He was gasping and choking, and we realized he had nearly suffocated. This event was so comprehensively stupid that it killed enthusiasm for the hideout, which was immediately abandoned.

Some years before this episode, "Cobby" and "Punchy" Swift had received for Christmas a dandy little 7-foot-long rowboat, and they used it on the creek, actually an estuary, that flowed through a salt marsh situated across the railroad tracks which bordered their folk's property. One day, when I was about fifteen, I saw that boat in Ducky Chipman's back yard, and noticed that the plywood sides were filled with small holes. The two boys had given the boat to Ducky after shooting it full of arrows. I bought the boat for about 50¢ and hauled it home on my brother's wooden wagon. Using plywood from my electric train board, I cut new sides, fitted them to the boat, and painted the whole thing green. Down Hollett Street and across the NY, NH & H railroad tracks lay upper reaches of a vast salt marsh, which is traversed by an estuary that fills and empties through a narrow rocky inlet at Cohasset harbor. When the tide in this creek was high, I'd load the boat onto the wagon, toss in homemade oars, and head to the creek to spend many happy hours poling or rowing my boat through the peaceful marshland. That little boat was of such simple construction that I decided to build another. Looking around our barn for suitable building materials, I spotted a large wooden organ pipe that had been salvaged during dismantling of the old First Baptist Church organ a few years earlier. Many neighborhood kids had got hold of a few of the smallest pipes, but someone had glommed onto this giant 5 footer, and eventually donated it for a church auction sale. I bought it for 25¢, and had to use exhaust from our vacuum cleaner in order to hear its deep-throated whistle. I took this large pipe to my attic workshop and cut the four sides apart with my small circular saw. Next, I laid the four pieces side by side, fastened them together with a few cross pieces, then cut the assembly into the shape of a boat bottom. I nailed on a stem, some ribs, and a transom, then added sides using the last lengths of plywood from my train board. Using roofing tar, I caulked the seams and next painted the boat brown. This little craft, all 5 feet of her, was just large enough to hold one person without capsizing, but at least I had succeeded in building a real boat. To get both boats to the creek in one trip, I put the smaller boat inside the larger one, and carried both on my brother's wagon. One grand project involved the use of both boats. On that occasion, I loaded the two onto the wagon, then filled the smaller boat with heavy rope, block and tackle, several lengths of 2x4, an axe, several stakes, and some lengths of pot warp (rope used in lobster fishing). After launching both boats, and towing the smaller one, I rowed downstream for about 3/4 mile to a point where the creek is perhaps 40 feet wide. There, I set up a 2x4 A frame on each bank, anchored each with a pair of deadmen, then tightly stretched a length of 3/4" manila rope (from Sears mail-order catalog) between the two. This rope was first threaded through a single-sheave pulley block that could thus travel to and fro along the rope. Next, a block and tackle was attached to the traveling block and the smaller boat was attached to the hook on the lowest pulley block. This arrangement enabled me to hoist the boat completely above water, with me in it, then use the traveling block to move the boat back and forth in the manner of a cable car. It worked! After crossing above the creek a few times, the entire assembly was dismantled, loaded into the smaller boat, and towed back to the launch site at Hollett Street. All of this took several hours, and was not attempted again.

Regarding the larger boat, one final episode is well worth recounting. One day, in the fall of 1944, I took the boat down to the creek in company of Paul "P" Miles. After launching the boat, Paul stepped in too far beyond the center line, capsized the boat and ended up soaking wet! We retrieved the boat, pulled it back home, and proceeded to get Paul dried out. He opened his wallet – I didn't even own one at the time – and laid out various cards, bills and photographs. He left one photo in the wallet saying that I wouldn't be allowed to see it. Curiosity caused me to snatch the wallet, run into the house, and up to my bedroom with Paul in hot pursuit. I locked the door and opened the wallet, revealing a photograph of a girl I didn't recognize. Coming out of the room, I handed Paul the wallet and asked who she was. He said, "Her name is Margie Macy, Tom's sister." Well, I had known Tom ever since early grade-school years, and had even been in his family's driveway during a scouting pickup. "Tom has a sister?" I asked. Paul answered, "Yes. In fact, he has two sisters." Little did I know it then, but the girl whose photo I had just seen would later become my wife – but that's another story!

Margie Macy, about whom I first learned when Paul Miles fell out of my boat. Photo: 1945.

# Chapter 8
## Family Outings And Other Travels

Growing up during the Great Depression had little meaning for kids such as me, who lived in comfortable homes, were well clothed, and were fed nourishing meals three times each day. Scituate was primarily a residential town, the principal local industries – sea mossing, lobster fishing, and truck gardening – being little affected by the economic downturn. Otherwise, the town's wage earners were businessmen, professionals, laborers, tradesmen, or in the service sector. Massive layoffs did not occur. Nonetheless, by the mid-thirties my family was struggling financially – four children, a substantial mortgage, need to purchase a new car – but I never considered us to be "poor." Looking back, the signs were certainly evident – Mom dyeing my outgrown mackinaw and giving it to my brother as a Christmas present; summer shoes (called Breezies) worn through at the sole and stuffed with cardboard inserts to prolong useful life; weekly dinners featuring tripe, cheese soufflé, or kidney stew; during hunting season dinners of rabbit, squirrel, and occasionally pheasant. I still think with revulsion of the thermo-electric shock produced in tooth fillings when biting down on a piece of buckshot within a chunk of fried squirrel meat!

Dad's position as manager of the Whiting Milk distribution plant on Gannett Road was demanding, especially during the summer season, but he did arrange a number of family outings, that is, until the outbreak of WWII. At least once each year, we drove to the end of Surfside Road, parked the car (no parking allowed there today!), climbed up the vast storm ridge of rounded pebbles and cobbles which mark Surfside Beach, and had an old-fashioned cookout. Arriving atop the ridge, we children scampered along the beach seeking driftwood, which Dad kindled into a fire with the aid of crumpled newspaper. Hamburgers comprised the main course, and these were cooked on a folding wire rack (which I still have) that was propped up on small piles of stone. Inserted into buns, together with a slice of onion and tomato, these were some of the most delicious burgers I have ever tasted, perhaps because some of the burning wood was coated with lead-based paint! Our beverage was homemade root beer or lemonade (also homemade), and dessert was ice cream, which on these occasions came from the Whiting Milk Company. At twilight, we scanned the horizon for the so-called "New York boat," a vessel known to pass our coast in the evening as it proceeded from Boston towards the Cape Cod Canal. Ablaze with lights, this beautiful ship was a sight we viewed many times, but I never wished myself aboard because of the unlikelihood of such an event, or having vivid memories of folks perishing aboard the steamer Morro Castle off the New Jersey coast in 1934. Less frequently, our family drove to the Cape Cod Canal (where two beautiful new bridges had recently been completed), built our usual fire and cooked our evening meal. Views from the bluff were, and still are, awe-inspiring, and we watched passing boats with the fascination typical of childhood innocence.

Twice, while I was very young, perhaps six or seven years old, we visited Benson's Wild Animal Farm in Hudson, NH.

Crew at Whiting Milk plant on Gannett Road, ca. 1940. Front row (l. to r.), Rennie Jacobucci, "Pooch" Dowd; back row: unknown, Frank Valine, Elizabeth Brady, Dad; driver unknown.

This was an especially memorable treat because there I had my first and only rides on an elephant. We probably saw many other animals, but I remember only the skeletal remains in a supposed Indian burial site and a very large stuffed gorilla.

Because of the busy summer season in Scituate, my dad could not take off any weekends until late in October. One such weekend involved a trip to Kittery, Maine, where we stayed overnight in a rustic cabin and ate dinner in a restaurant which boasted an ugly boar's head with red electric lights for eyes. Pretty scary! On another such occasion, over Halloween weekend, we drove up to North Woodstock, NH, where we stayed for two nights in another of those rustic cabins so typical of pre-war northern New England. From North Woodstock, we toured all the local attractions – The Flume, The Basin, Old Man of the Mountain (collapsed in 2003) and Echo Lake. One evening, while dining in a North Woodstock restaurant, an obviously drunk man approached Dad from the bar area and asked if he could "talk to your girls." Presumably, he wanted to ask their preference for a jukebox song, but Dad got very angry and cried, "No! Go back where you belong," whereupon the fellow slunk back to his corner table. This was one of only three or four times when I got a glimpse of my father's temper. On the day we started for home, we stopped at the Polar Caves, near Plymouth, NH, this attraction actually being closed for the winter. Strangely, the gate was not chained tightly shut, so we eased through it and took a self-guided tour through the jumble of glacial boulders, which just happened to have enough interconnected spaces to make for a really nifty transit. I remember particularly a very narrow passageway called the "lemon squeezer," and the very cold air of the "caves."

These trips were short, but left lasting impressions. The latter ended on a sour note because we were absent from Scituate over Halloween, and arrived home to find all our clotheslines cut, and the glass windows of our "hut" smashed! The police inquired around the neighborhood, decided who they *thought* had participated, and made each of a number of kids pony up $1.65 to replace the damaged property. My good friend Gray Curtis was one of those required to pay even though, as he related many years later, he had no part in the vandalism. One can imagine how the kids who had to pay felt about children of the Hattin family!

Each year during the 1930's and early 1940's, one of our longest outings was a trip to Pomfret Center, CT, to visit our Hattin relatives. The distance was about 90 miles, and the route mostly tortuous, with travel time being about three hours. On such trips, we always carried an enameled metal pan because I tended to get car sick, and usually did. On this long trip we invariably played games in order to pass the time. Because of slow driving speeds, tallying license plates on passing cars from different states was easy. Counting points for various animal sightings was another favorite, with one team covering the right hand side, the other covering the left. We counted 1 point for each chicken, 2 points for a dog or cat, 5 points each for cows, 10 points for a horse (beginning to be scarce by then), and 25 points for a cat seen in a window. We traveled by way of Wrentham, thence southwestwardly into Rhode Island, passing my mother's childhood home in West Wrentham while en route. A point of fascination was Grants Mills, RI, a company town of worker's modest yellow-clapboard homes and large mill buildings, followed by Rhode Island towns with funny-sounding names such as Chepachet and Woonsocket.[1]

In addition to seeing and staying with Grandma Hattin and exploring a gigantic barn situated next door to her farm, visits to Pomfret Center, CT, were made exciting by our impish

---

[1] In the spring of 1997, Marge and I traveled throughout Great Britain with our Scituate friends, Gray and Jean Curtis. One B&B was presided over by a friendly lady who told me she had been to the U.S.– specifically, to Chepachet, RI. A week later and many miles away we had dinner in a pub whose landlord kept a record of foreign visitors. After "signing in" we turned his log to the preceding page and found the names of a couple from – you guessed it – Chepachet, RI!!

male cousins, Irvie and Ronnie Hattin. Together, we climbed a giant beech tree adjacent to the railroad station, clambered over piles of freshly cut planks in the lumber yard across the street from their home, and jumped off a railroad bridge into an impossibly shallow stream. Uncle Irvin's Red and White store carried all manner of merchandise – boots, gaiters, ammunition, cookware, shovels, etc. – in addition to a full line of groceries, produce, and meat. Around the Fourth of July, the store carried a wide assortment of fireworks, including many highly explosive types. One such was a sort of torpedo which could be attached to an automobile tire in such a way as to simulate a blowout. Once, I saw Uncle Irvin place one of these on each of a customer's car tires. When the car was moved, all four went off with a huge "bang," but the driver did not see the humor in this prank! Uncle Irvin, a colorful character who once served on the Connecticut State Legislature, had a Model A Ford coupe which he had meticulously hand painted to a like-new finish. In this, we drove to his 20-acre property in Baker Hollow, right in the middle of a Connecticut state forest. On an old farmhouse foundation he had built a rustic but lovely cabin, which was illuminated by gasoline lanterns and heated by a stone fireplace. Some yards from the house were two privies, one labeled "Pointers" and the other labeled "Setters." Water had to be fetched from a spring situated some distance from the house, and wood for the fireplace was cut by a local hermit named Joel. Happy were the days we spent at this special retreat – Hattin's Hideaway.

Mom had a cousin named Marion Gare whose husband, Ed, was proprietor of the E.J. Gare and Son jewelry store in Northampton, MA. For several summers they rented a charming lakeside cottage in the little town of Goshen, which is situated in beautiful hill country about 20 miles northwest of their home. Together with their three children, Luther, Jessie and John, the family vacationed far from the cares of everyday

Uncle Irvin Hattin and family on porch of Hattin's Red and White Store, Pomfret Center, CT, ca. 1943. Left to right: Ronnie, Uncle Irvin, Ann Marie, Irvie, Aunt Ann.

living. In 1939, I was invited to join them for a week of fun in the sun and on the water, and could hardly believe my good fortune.

When the departure day arrived, I was driven to Boston by my parents, and with little ado, placed on a bus of the Peter Pan line for travel alone to Northampton. Interestingly, the route was not direct, but dipped southward to Stafford Springs, CT, possibly so Peter Pan could qualify as an interstate carrier. (The Peter Pan bus line was still in existence as recently as summer, 2005!) From the bus window, I waved a bit forlornly to my mother, and settled in for a long, lonely ride to a point farther west than I had ever been previously. Cousin Marion met me in Northampton, and after an overnight at their home, we were on

The author, headed for Northampton, MA, to visit the Gare family, 1939.

our way to the cottage. I was to have my own room, and was very comfortable there. All meals were prepared at the cottage, but most activity took place in or on the water. Two boats were at our disposal – a nice little white sailing dinghy and a heavy red rowboat which a neighbor girl, Jane Wragg, and I christened "the red ugly." Luther had a summer job, but when at the cabin took me under his wing and taught me how to sail. After hoisting the single sail, we tacked slowly to the upper end of the lake. There, Luther let out the sail, remarking as it billowed under pressure of the wind, "Here we go, like a bat out of hell." Sure enough, we did, and quickly reached the lake's lower limit. I was entranced by Luther's grownupness. Imagine, using a word such as "hell" without getting your mouth washed with Fels Naptha soap! Language aside, he became a good companion and energetic mentor.

Inside the cabin, we played games during evenings, and I played the Victrola, soon discovering a ragtime piece entitled "Draggin' the Dragon." This kind of music was new to me, and I played that record over and over and over. My Goshen visit was for just one week, and before I knew it the week had passed. All too soon my folks arrived to take me home. While everyone was saying goodbye, I ran into the house, wound up the Victrola, and started playing "Draggin' the Dragon." I wanted this to be my final memory of the place. We loaded up the car, and just before leaving I dashed back into the cabin yet again to hear the tune for a final, final time. Alas, the Gare's were so sick of hearing the record that the machine had already been turned off. They had indulged me long enough!

By far, the most exciting of our travels, and that for which the recollections are so vivid, was our 1940 trip to the New York World's Fair. My parents and sisters had made the trip in 1939, but my brother was too young that year, so the trip was repeated the following year, with all of us "on board." Once in Flushing, Long Island, scene of the fair, we stayed for the duration at a reasonably priced guest house, taking our breakfasts at a diner and our dinners in various restaurants. The fair itself was truly mind boggling. From the signature Trylon and Perisphere to the exhibits of corporations and governments, everything was unbelievably wonderful and amazing in the eyes of an eleven-year-old. Most memorable was the General Motors exhibit, "The World of Tomorrow," which we viewed from moving chairs. From above, we looked down on complex models of futuristic cities and complex layouts of multi-laned highways that were complete with moving traffic – teardrop-shaped cars, etc. – and cloverleaf intersections which one could hardly imagine would ever really come into existence. These miniature highways were a preview of our present-day interstates. The General Electric exhibit featured Steinmetz Hall, where simulations of electrical storms included thunder and huge arcs of man-made "lightning." In another exhibit we saw an Egyptian mummy, which was viewed first with all its wrappings, then by fluoroscopy. B.F. Goodrich featured their "Safety Arena," where Jimmy Lynch's automobile stunts were amazing – cars driving up ramps at great speeds and "flying" through the air above other cars, and being driven on just two wheels instead of four. Among other things, the railroad exhibit displayed the oldest U.S. locomotive. In the evening, the tune *Finlandia* floated gently through the deepening twilight. Of course, we visited an exhibit in the Perisphere, which was similar to, though less impressive than, the G.M. show. The Japanese exhibit included a pearl-encrusted liberty bell symbolizing peace, a bit of irony as December 7, 1941, was soon to prove. Our last day in New York was highlighted by a trip up the Empire State Building and eating a scrumptious meal in an amazingly inexpensive Chinese restaurant – huge amounts of food served in metals bowls which came with a metal cover. This seemed the best Chinese dinner I would ever eat. On our final morning, we ate at our usual diner where our waiter, who reminded us of Jimminy Cricket, impressed all of us when placing our orange juice order by calling out, "six O.J.!" This was also the place where I first heard the term "over easy." I hated to leave, and the trip home has been completely forgotten, probably because I was worn out and slept almost all the way.

War clouds and eventual onset of World War II put an end to family travels, and by the end of that terrible conflict my mother was suffering from the cancer which took her life at age forty nine.

In the summer of 1946, "Sarge" Bartlett and I concocted a scheme to climb Mt. Washington, New England's highest peak, and spend some time on the Appalachian Trail. Each of us had purchased a WWII tubular-framed knapsack into which we packed all of our gear. Unbelievably, most of our food consisted of canned goods such that our bulging packs seemingly weighed a ton – we had shunned most perishables, and had yet to hear of freeze-dried trail food. With a beginning lift from Sarge's stepfather, we started off in high spirits, and by early afternoon had reached Pinkham Notch. There, starting from the Appalachian Mountain Club lodge, we began ascent to Tuckerman Ravine.[2]

---

[2] Both of us been there previously with a scout group headed by Ward C. "Pa" Swift, Sr. (See chapter on boy scouting).

*Donald E. Hattin*

The author, with heavily loaded Army knapsack, on southern flank of Mt. Washington, NH, 1946.

Upon reaching this famous cirque, we proceeded up the much steeper Lion's Head trail. After considerable effort, we reached the ravine's lip and then continued upgrade on the gentler, boulder-strewn slope which flanks the Mt. Washington summit. By the time we had hiked another mile, Sarge declared that he was "bushed," so we decided to camp right there on the unsheltered slope. For supper, we set up my small Sterno stove, heated up a couple cans of beans, made some sandwiches, drank some water, and called it a day. By this time, the sun had set and night was fast closing in. We unrolled our sleeping bags on some fairly rough ground, of which there was plenty all around, and were soon asleep.

No one had told us that weather conditions on the mountain can be exceedingly treacherous, and that snow can fall on any day of the year. But then, hardly anyone had been informed of our purpose or destination, and we optimistically assumed that the weather would be fine. Neither of us had any garment warmer than a sweatshirt, and neither of us had brought a hat or poncho! The temperature did drop, but the sky remained mercifully clear and we awoke to a cool but beautifully sunny morning. Had we awakened to snowfall, fog or heavy rain, we would have had more than a little trouble locating the Appalachian Trail, with possibility of some pretty severe consequences. *I* wouldn't go so far as to say we had been foolish, but without question we had been outstandingly foolish! Although the summit was only a mile or so from our camp, Sarge was feeling unwell, so, after a spartan breakfast, we hiked over to the A.T., descended past Lake of the Clouds and its attendant hut, and continued on a downward course toward the valley of Crawford Notch. With sun shining brightly and temperature rising into the 60's, our adventure took on a distinctly pleasurable turn. Well below timberline, we suddenly encountered a stylishly outfitted thirtyish woman who was actually *ascending* the trail. Her dressy clothing and shiny shoes were hardly proper hiking gear, and so outrageously out of place that we could but wonder what she was doing here and where she was headed. We sat while she asked the distance to Lake of the Clouds hut, and when we replied she said, "I was told it was only a couple of hours flat walking," but she decided to continue, and departed without further comment. Sarge opined that the only rational explanation of her appearance and destination was that she practiced the world's oldest profession, and planned to ply her trade at the hut. We would never discover the truth.

Following departure of the mystery woman, Sarge and I continued down the A.T. to the valley floor. Once on the highway, we hiked a couple more miles and came upon a group of tourist cabins. We forked over the required $6.00, deciding to rent a unit despite a sign at the entrance which read "Gentiles Only." Well, previous to that moment, I had never heard the word "gentiles," but realized immediately that some particular group of folks was being excluded. For the second time in my life, I was experiencing what could only be some kind of racist/ethnic act, and found such exclusion repulsive. Had dusk not been approaching, and had we been less tired, we may well have tried to find a more welcoming hostel. To this day I regret having patronized that place.

On the following morning, after eating cold food from our dwindling larder, Sarge and I hit the highway and headed south. Having no immediate success in hitching a ride, Sarge kneeled with hands clasped as if in prayer while I displayed an earnest thumb. Surprisingly, the very next car stopped, and a very pretty young (thirtyish) lady motioned us into the vehicle. She admitted that Sarge's prayerful pose had done the trick, and after asking where we were headed, started south toward Boston. Being low on fuel, she pulled into a gas station (one pump, full service) where a uniformed attendant asked, "Five gallons?" WWII was by now long ended, and gasoline had finally become abundant, so she replied, "No, I'll just use those magical words 'fill her up!'" Our trip was over, and we were now a little older and hopefully a little bit wiser.

# Chapter 9
## Grandparents

**Chester Grandparents**

Once or twice a year we traveled to Wrentham, MA, to visit Grandpa and Grandma Chester and my mother's half sister, Ruth Gilpatrick, and her family. Mother's dad was Fenner Eliab Whipple, a Mayflower descendant, who was born in Cumberland, RI, on February 21, 1863, and died in Philadelphia on April 17, 1898. He had married my maternal grandmother, Anna Elizabeth Murray, in Camden, NJ, on April 2, 1890. She was born on October 2, 1870, in Sandusky, OH, the daughter of John Murray (a Civil War veteran) and Bridgett Meenan. Fenner and Anna had two children – Ralph Whipple, who became a geologist and taught at Marietta College, OH, for 35 years, and Una Vestella Whipple, my mother. After Fenner's death, Anna married Theodore Chester, the step-grandfather of my boyhood memories. How and where Anna met Theodore is a mystery, but their married life was spent in Wrentham, MA, where he was station agent for the New York, New Haven, and

Hartford Railroad. I knew him only as a retired gentleman who, though only in his sixties, always seemed very old to my inexpert eyes. He and Grandma Chester lived comfortably in a rented, two story home on Shears Street, which she once told me cost only $15 or $20 per month! Theodore retired with a railroad pension, that being their primary source of income. Because of his truly superior penmanship, he augmented his income by doing specialized writing, but such work was not a long-term arrangement. Vegetable gardening added substantially to their resources. Grandpa rented some ground on an adjacent property, and raised such crops as corn, beets, carrots, radishes, lettuce, peas, pole beans and more. A series of cold frames enabled him to start plants early in the growing season, and results of his efforts were substantial. Root crops were stored in their cellar for winter use by burying carrots, beets, etc., in sand held in a stack of square wooden bushel boxes.

The cellar also contained Grandpa's workshop, comprising bench and old-fashioned hand tools. Using these, he made for me a marvelous little round-bottomed boat fashioned from a 12" length of log that had been cut in half lengthwise and hollowed out with hammer and chisel. This little craft had bluff bows, two seats, a small mast, and a sail. Painted red, that wonderful boat floated on an even keel, a feature which

Grandfather Theodore Chester performing his duties as station agent at Wrentham, MA, ca. 1920.

Grandpa Chester holding my sister, Betty, 1926. In this image he appears essentially as known to the author.

must have cost him no little effort. One of his triumphs was a square-legged, rectangular footstool which he constructed for my mother. The stool was complete with mortised horizontal stretchers and cross braces, and served our family throughout my boyhood. Often, Grandpa Chester would mend things such as loose chair spindles by means of animal-hoof or animal-hide glue, which came in small rectangular sheets that had to be dissolved in water. The resulting syrup-like glue worked well enough, but had an odor offensive enough to repel skunks. And, speaking of odors, the Chester living room smelled always of stale pipe tobacco smoke. There, beside his favorite easy chair, was a smoking stand on which were arranged several of Grandpa's pipes – briar and corncob – and a tin of Edgeworth. So persistent was his smoking habit that each pipe contained a cake so thick that he could scarcely insert his little finger to tamp the tobacco. Over and over he would light up, and puff contentedly while reading the daily newspaper. He used large wooden kitchen matches, and the best part was that to me fell the honor of blowing out the flame – heady stuff for a boy not yet six years old.

Grandma Chester was a petite, sprightly, quick-witted lady who seemed to spend most of her time in the kitchen. That room featured a large cast-iron stove, a wall-mounted coffee grinder, and a soapstone sink. Her pantry always smelled of apple pie. It seemed to me that she was always cooking, and the aromas of good food pervaded her domain most of the day. Her white hair, usually done up in a bun, actually manifested several decades of growth, and fell well below her waist when let down. After Theodore died, in 1936, she took up cigarette smoking, and spent part of each afternoon sitting in the dining room on her "thinking stool," the butt in her mouth being smoked so short that she held the final half inch on one prong of a hairpin. Her telephone, an oak box with ringer bells and a hand crank, was attached to one wall of that room. She was

Grandmother Anna Murray Whipple Chester (right), with her daughter, Ruth, my mom's half sister, ca. 1920.

on a three-party line, and the number of rings signaled whose call was coming in. Grandma thrived on gossip, learning some from listening in on other folks' conversations (many people did this), or by talking to Geneva, the telephone operator, who also "listened in" and was a fountain of juicy information. When relating some of the local "news," Grandma's eyes twinkled because this was a major entertainment of her widowhood.

After Grandpa Chester's death, Grandma walked the considerable distance to Wrentham town center, where she always shopped at the Cash and Carry grocery store. When visiting, I loved to walk there with her. Only later did I discover that at some stores a running tally of purchases could be made, the cumulative bill being paid weekly. But *not* at a store with the name "Cash and Carry!" After my mother's early demise, it was Grandma Chester who decreed that Mom's sterling dinnerware should be mine, and fifty seven years later, we still use it on all formal occasions.

## Hattin Grandparents

Born Louisa Maria Zoller in 1870, my paternal grandmother was brought up in a Brooklyn, NY, orphanage because her father's death left her mother, Marie Antoinetta (Robinson) Zoller unable to provide for her two children (Louisa and Edward). I know little of her growing years, but a some point, she met and married my grandfather, Gono Hattin, who was born in Chaplin, Connecticut, in 1870. I remember grandpa Hattin only as a man in his sixties, bedridden following a severe stroke, and also afflicted with diabetes. He was born to a farming family and lived on Tower Hill Farm, Chaplin, Connecticut, until adulthood. His principal occupations were U.S. Government meat inspector, at least partly in the greater New York City area (where he probably met my grandmother), and later, for most of his working years, as owner/operator of general stores in Eastford and Pomfret Center, Connecticut. I have images of both stores, the first sporting a sign, "L.M. HATTIN STORE," the second replete with sign plus gravity-feed-type Gulf gasoline pump. Before Grandpa Hattin's death, the business had been assumed by my Uncle Irvin Hattin, and they traded houses – Grandma and Grandpa moving from an apartment above the store to a farmhouse about half a mile away. And what a great place that was for our occasional visits to Pomfret Center.

The farmhouse was white, had a front-facing gabled wing with living room, dining room, den, and two upstairs bedrooms, and to the right as one faced the house, a section with kitchen, pantry, and laundry. A shed piled high with stove wood lay off the laundry, and a detached garage lay to the right of and close to the house. Out back, there was a chicken coop, and off to the right of the garage was a small barn. The section of house having the kitchen was fronted by a sheltered porch from which the view over the adjacent valley was truly beautiful and peaceful. Above the kitchen were two bedrooms – the second had to be entered via the first, which was the larger of the two.

I remember spending many happy days at this house, early on when my cousins still lived there, but mostly when Grandma Hattin was there. The pantry was a wonderful place – large, and always smelling of pies! An old-fashioned egg scale was used to size eggs that my grandmother sold when she still had lots of hens. The kitchen was fitted with a classic cast-iron wood

L.M. Hattin store in Pomfret Center, CT, ca. 1935. Gasoline was hand pumped upward into glass cylinder, and delivered to automobile tank by gravity. Gasoline was 17.3¢ per gallon.

stove, with a firebox at the left beneath two cast-iron lids, and an oven at the right. The heat from this stove rose through a ceiling register to warm the larger of the two bedrooms above. I always seemed to sleep in that room while visiting, and was awakened each morning by sounds of Grandma stoking the stove – lids off, wood being added to rekindle the previous night's fire, the lids clanging down, and a little grate shaking. This routine was followed unfailingly, summer and winter. All of this took place at dawn because Grandma was an early riser, and always cooked a large and very satisfying breakfast. As soon as everyone was dressed, we'd gather in the toasty warm kitchen and sit at the old-fashioned table for a real down-home meal. Oatmeal, milk, and sugar came first, with orange juice, of course. This was followed by bacon, eggs, toast and jelly. I can still smell the woody aroma of that magical place. The dishes were washed in a large soapstone sink. Up on the window ledge was a blue glass Shirley Temple pitcher, which is now happily displayed in my own home. When Grandma was older, her brother Ed came to dine at the farm. He spent all day sitting in that kitchen, using a pressed back, armchair-type rocker that has also passed to my possession. As I write this (1992), 120 years after Grandma's birth, that chair is being used in the home of my elder daughter, Sandy.

On to the dining room, where dinner was always served. At one end, toward the center of the house, the dining room floor featured a huge round grate which admitted heat for the entire "living" part of the house. A chain-operated arrangement allowed control of the damper, which was closed at night and opened in the morning. As Grandma grew to old age, Uncle Irvin came over daily to fire the furnace, this job becoming my dad's when he moved to Connecticut to live with and care for his mother after my mom's death. Dinners in the living room were simple, but elegant – roasts of beef, turkey at Thanksgiving, chicken or pork, and always mashed potatoes. Sometimes we'd have other vegetables, but carrots seemed to be the favorite. Knives and forks were laid by the plates, but spoons were displayed in a small, tall, ornamented glass dish. It, too, has found its way into my home, and I treasure it for evoking memories of laughter, story telling, and hearty meals. It was at the dining room table that Grandma presented me with a large number of family photographs and told me who the people were, where they had lived, who they had married, what children they had raised and when they had died. She was a fountain of information, even in her eighties and nineties, and I wrote down everything she told me. I still have the pictures and notes.

The living room was quite long, and had as its most attractive item a magnificent pump organ complete with mirror and candle stands on the upper part. Very Victorian, very playable. I'll always remember the name of one key in particular – "diapasin." I never did know what that meant, but I loved to pull all the stops in and out as I played chopsticks or anything else I'd ever learned about a keyboard (which wasn't very much). My sister, Marjorie, was married in that living room in 1947, I believe, and she dearly loved that organ. The whole thing was checked before the wedding, and a local woman, Annie Ash,

Grandmother Louisa Zeller Hattin, ca. 1950.

was prevailed upon to play. I attended the wedding, of course, and afterward had a hair-raising ride to Scituate with my cousin, Henry. He had a WWII jeep, and with the top down, 40 mph seemed like a hundred. My rush to get home that night was occasioned by plans to take my future wife, Margie Macy, to a senior prom or some other school-related dance. But this is a real aside, and here's another. When Grandma became too old to live at the farmhouse, she moved to her daughter's house in Scituate, Massachusetts, and later to Henry's house in Norwell, Massachusetts, where her daughter, Edith (Henry's mother), was also to live and look out for her. At that time, Grandma gave the organ to my sister, who, unable at the time to transport it to her home, put it in storage. Several years later, after they had moved to Chicago, Marge's husband failed to pay the storage charge one year, and the organ apparently was sold at a warehouse auction. Oh, me! Oh, my! I've often thought of the trouble and effort I'd have undertaken to keep that wonderful heirloom in the family. The cost of transport seems so trivial in comparison to the price of losing a family treasure. But I digress.

The den had a wonderful centerpiece – the stuffed head and antlers of a deer that Grandpa Hattin had shot many years earlier. The head was so old and dry that the nose had cracked open, and Grandma had tied a small white bag there to catch the stuffing (sawdust, I think) as it trickled out. On the wall hung a neat .22-caliber Winchester Special octagon-barrel pump-action repeating rifle. Years later, Dad gave me that rifle, and I have it still. Called a "carnival gun" because of its common use at shooting galleries, the ammunition is now hard to find, but I've got three nearly full boxes, two of which are at least seventy five years old!

Upstairs was not too interesting. My grandmother's bedroom had boxy oak furniture, and the wall nearest the chimney was streaked with soot caused by rain coming through the leaky flue. "My" bedroom was cold at night, but comfortably warm after Grandma got the morning stove fired up. I still used this room during visits after being married, and always slept soundly because the entire home was so quiet of an evening. Waking up was partly a matter of hearing the stove being worked, and partly owing to the crowing of a banty rooster which occupied a coop just behind the house.

As kids, we played on the porch, in the barn, and on the hillside behind the house. This hillside rose to a railroad track of the New York, New Haven and Hartford Railroad. A stream passed under the track and across an upper corner of Grandma's pasture. Across the track was a large, round-topped hill which was part pasture, part woods. The view from the top was breathtaking, even in the eyes of a kid like me who rarely paid much attention to scenery. A larger stream (perhaps the same one) crossed a meadow that lay in the opposite direction, downhill from the farmhouse and across the secondary highway that skirted Grandma's property. One day, I took off with a fishing pole and worms that Grandma had furnished. I fished the stream for about a half hour, catching one small fish about 4 inches long and slender as a woman's thumb. Grandma told me it was a "dace." I think that day deterred me from further interest in freshwater fishing because I've done very little of it since.

One of the greatest adventures we had at the farm was when my cousins, Irvie and Ronnie, had come over from their home above my uncle's store (by then known as "Hattin's Red and White Store." We climbed into the very narrow space between the house and garage, assembled kindling and wood sticks into a suitable pile, and started a fire. It wasn't long before Grandma caught a whiff of the smoke, and came running out of the house in a regular tizzy. You can imagine the dressing down all of us got; our fire could easily have caused both garage and house to burn to the ground.

How many times I visited that farmhouse I can't say, probably only once a year as a child because it was 90 miles from our Scituate home, and the route between Scituate and Pomfret Center was complicated and the roads pretty torturous. I think it took 3 hours to get there. One of the last overnight visits was with my new bride while on our way to Kansas in 1950. She cried all day as we departed New England. To please her, I would have turned back, but she said to press on, and to my everlasting gratitude, we did.

# Chapter 10
## Aunt Millie And Uncle Bud

If ever there was a topic for inclusion in this volume, Aunt Millie and Uncle Bud Cummings fill the bill. In every respect they were "larger than life," having experienced enough excitement and adventure to satisfy the most restless members of their generation.

Aunt Millie Hattin was born in Warrenville, CT, on August 16, 1907, but spent the latter part of her girlhood in Pomfret Center. From earliest years into her seventies she was what is known as a "looker," not only knowing this to be a fact but also flaunting her beauty with neither restraint nor modesty. Always the practical joker, she spiked the punch at a high school dance and admitted it to the principal – who had promised expulsion if he caught the culprit – on graduation day! Following high school she enrolled in a Boston hairdressing school, reaching that city on class days via the New York, New Haven, and Hartford Railroad. Pomfret station was just steps from the family home, and trainmen were eager to see her mischievous face each day. On more than one occasion, she reached the station seconds late only to have an ever-alert conductor signal the engineer to stop the train and back up! Aunt Millie grew to expect that kind of adoration, receiving it willingly and sometimes laughingly throughout her long and interesting life. How and where she met her future husband, Prescott B. "Bud" Cummings, is something I never learned, but meet they did and marry they would. Their wedding took place on November 17, 1928, in The Little Church Around the Corner in New York City.

Uncle Bud was the grandson of Charles S. Cummings and son of Frank A. Cummings, who, with his cousin Benjamin,[1] were proprietors of a well-known wholesale and retail grocery in New Bedford, MA. Shortly after his marriage, Uncle Bud discovered that a family member had purchased an Eastham, MA, property comprising about 30 acres and a long unused Cape Cod-style cottage, which much later was discovered to have been constructed in 1680. No one in the family wanted the place – the outer Cape not yet having attracted many sum-

---

[1]Benjamin F. Cummings was part owner of the Charles W. Morgan, which is the only surviving square-rigged wooden American whaleship, during its last voyage. Uncle Bud was at the dock in 1921 when the Morgan discharged her final cargo of whale oil.

mer residents. Upon seeing the property; house, outbuildings, and land; Aunt Millie exclaimed that the place reminded her of the Warrenville farmhouse and decided that this is where she and Uncle Bud should spend their lives. (Great choice, Aunt Millie.)

Upon his father's death, Uncle Bud had inherited $10,000, and also had income from the Cummings Trust. Noting that fishing and turnip farming were principal industries around

Aunt Mildred Hattin Cummings, 1964.

Uncle Prescott B. "Bud" Cummings, 1955.

Eastham, he determined to become a fisherman, and for that purpose purchased a large boat. Before he could arrange insurance, the boat caught fire and burned to the waterline. This occurred during Prohibition, and opportunity thus presented itself to recoup his loss by involving himself in the highly profitable trade of rumrunning. All of this happened before I was old enough to appreciate Uncle Bud's efforts on behalf of the drinking public, which on Cape Cod was most of the public. In the 1980's, Bud was asked by the Eastham Historical Society to record an oral history of his days as a bootlegger, and the story is recounted as a chapter in the book *Growing Up on Cape Cod* by Don Sparrow (1999). At $5 per case of booze, Uncle Bud garnered plenty of spending money from this enterprise.

When prohibition ended, Uncle Bud tried turnip farming – a big thing on the Cape in those days – but too many turnips translated to low prices so he turned to fishing. Rising early, getting onto the water before his pals, and staying out late even in wintertime, he did quite well because fish always brought good prices. Looking toward real riches, however, Uncle Bud and Aunt Millie turned their attention to Alaska, which had attracted her interest for several years. There, they could make their fortune in gold mining. Although the whole scheme had originated with Aunt Millie, she did not participate in the first trip, which began in April, 1940, and as consolation took the first of what would become many trips to Mexico. Uncle Bud and his partners soon realized that to be successful in the area they planned to mine, they needed a hydraulic operation, that is, washing large volumes of river gravel through sluice boxes by means of a high-pressure water line and fire-hose-like nozzle.

Our family was agog to learn about this daring venture, and was breathless to learn more about that extremely distant land. On the first trip, Uncle Bud and his partners crossed the country by bus. For the second and longer lasting trip, he and Aunt Millie purchased a new Chevrolet, which they left in Seattle pending return from the gold field. With a mountain of food and equipment, including water pipe, nozzles, cooking and eating utensils, warm clothing, a forge, tools, tar paper, oakum to chink their proposed cabin, and various weaponry, they left Seattle on August 22, 1941, on the steamer *Columbia* and proceeded to Valdez. From there they continued northward by truck to Chistochina, from which a tractor train would haul their supplies to the mine on Eagle Creek. Bud and Millie continued by truck to Gakona, and then flew from there to Eagle Creek. Two of the partners already had cabins; Bud and Millie built a third of spruce logs, with final dimensions being 16 by 20 feet. The tarpapered roof was covered with sod, and it was in this building that they spent the winter of 1941/1942.

Pipe for the hydraulic mining arrived tardily, but eventually the 2000-foot-long system was installed and washing of gravel progressed. Uncle Bud told me later that they washed a cubic yard per minute and retrieved about $1 in gold for each cubic yard. This sounds like a large amount of money in a hurry, but large boulders gradually obstructed operations, which often had to be shut down for several days while dynamite and sledge hammers were used to clear the way for more washing.

Japanese attacks on the Aleutian Islands brought an end to Uncle Bud and Aunt Millie's mining, which was just marginally profitable, so they abandoned the mine and returned to Eastham. All of my family members were awed by the harrowing exploits of their daring Alaskan adventures, involving bizarre encounters with large animals, a new rifle which wouldn't shoot straight, frostbite, a blood-poisoning incident, and much more.[2] Several large gold nuggets deriving from their mining exploits were brought home, and later incorporated into an impressively heavy watch chain – a fitting memento of that remarkable journey.

Shortly after their return to the Cape, my brother and I were invited to spend a week with Aunt Millie and Uncle Bud, who had returned to fishing for a living. He had a 16' catboat pow-

---

[2] The tale of their Alaskan adventures was told by Aunt Millie in a nearly 100-page letter which she sent home early in 1942. With it she included a long list of names (and addresses) of persons to whom the letter was to be successively forwarded. After we had read and forwarded it, the letter was "lost." In amazing detail, Aunt Millie reconstructed the letter 50 years later, when she was in her eighties!

ered by a Model A Ford engine; one day he took us fishing in Cape Cod Bay, and on another day clamming on Billingsgate Island. That island had served in practice bombing runs by our air forces, and the remains of dummy bombs were abundant. In fact, many Eastham homeowners used them as lawn decorations, most of which were painted in bright colors. We returned from Billingsgate with a large supply of clams and we put them in a cage in Salt Pond. On the following day, Russell and I put the clams in tin pails (gallon pails I believe), and peddled them throughout the Nauset Road neighborhood at 50¢ per container. No trouble getting rid of those sweet delicacies! During our visit, Uncle Bud decided to let me drive a stripped down Model A Ford which he used as a tractor. With motor running, me behind the wheel, Russell sitting on a wooden box beside me, the throttle lever set, and Uncle Bud's hand on the clutch, he indicated trails and lanes we could follow and said, "If you get in trouble, just turn off the ignition key." Then he let out the clutch and away we went at what seemed a dizzying speed. First I steered the vehicle down a trail in the woods, circled around some trees, came back past the house, sped down the driveway towards the road, and turned off on a side lane. Negotiating a loop counterclockwise at the lane's end brought near disaster, because the box on which Russell sat was not fastened. Tilting to the right, it almost dumped him onto the ground. Had this happened, he almost certainly would have been run over by the right rear wheel. The gas tank was very low on fuel to begin with, and the old Model A eventually came to a stop on its own. Good thing, too, because another few tight turns might have found Russell covered with tread marks. All this at the ages of ten and thirteen!

During 1942, the Bethlehem Steel Corporation established a new shipbuilding yard in Hingham, and it seemed that anyone who could lift a thumbtack was hired in some capacity. Many of the men were 4-F's, which meant they had some physical defect such as poor eyesight, deafness, etc., and Uncle Bud was one of those not subject to the draft. The shipyard offered good, steady wages and Bud hastened to the hiring office. Asked if he could read blueprints, he said, "Sure can," and was assigned a job in one of the shipways, starting on the following day. That night, in Eastham, he asked a carpenter friend to teach him the art of blueprint reading and began his shipyard duties the next day. Across the street from our home was the former home of Ben Young, which had become a rental property that had recently been vacated by George Burrill, retiring principal of Hatherly School. The Cummings moved in, and for a few weeks were our neighbors. Then they discovered a fine place on Hatherly Road that overlooked Musquashcut Pond and came with a rowboat. I loved rowing, and frequently rode my bike to their home, borrowed the boat, and rowed across the pond to the long ridge of cobbles known as Surfside Beach. Because of ship sinkings offshore, as well as feverish activity in the shipyards, all kinds of neat stuff came ashore, and I had soon transported a large stash of usable boards over the pond to my aunt and uncle's house. I never carried this lumber home on my bike, and never asked Aunt Millie to do so. Boating and collecting was the real fun.

One day, Uncle Bud's shipyard boss came to him and said, "Henry Kaiser just launched a Liberty ship in seven days. I want you to beat him." The shipyard produced LST's and destroyer escorts, and it was one of the latter which it was Bud's task to build in a hurry. Uncle Bud told me that during construction the ship grew like a thing alive, all the basic materials arriving in numbered pieces. With thousands of men and women on the job, sections of keel, ribs, plating, decking, bulkheads, etc. were hoisted into place and immediately welded together. Uncle Bud was on the job without sleep for five and a half days, at the end of which the DE slid down the shipway and erased Mr. Kaiser's record. Of course, a launched ship was hardly battle-ready. There remained the installation of power plants,

*Tales of a New England Boyhood*

electrical systems, controls, armament, anchors and chains, galley equipment, bunks and a myriad of other equipment, all of which took several weeks. Even so, the speed at which the work was done explains how the U.S. produced so many thousands of vessels in little more than three and a half years before V.J. Day, 1945. Uncle Bud received a plaque-mounted citation for his contribution.

With war over, the Hingham shipyard quickly shut down and the Cummings returned to their ancient Cape Cod cottage in Eastham. There, Bud became a building contractor, eventually constructing more than 400 homes and businesses in Eastham, Orleans, and Wellfleet. On the farm, he constructed two rental cottages, and converted a 250-year-old chicken coop into a third rental property. Of all the things he had raised on the farm, these buildings were the only things that ever produced a livable income. Little wonder that for the rest of their days, they called the place "Cottage Farm."[3]

---

[3] Bud and Millie's cottage, now 326 years old, was willed to Uncle Bud's niece, and therefore has now been in the family for 88 years!

The Cummings' cottage, built 1680, Eastham, MA. Left to right: Aunt Millie, Dad, Grandma Hattin, 1949. The ell was added early in the 18th century.

# Chapter 11
## Around The Neighborhood

**Historic Buildings**

From my earliest years in Scituate I was made aware, or on my own became aware, of the many historic sites and buildings for which the town is or should be noted. In 1936, Scituate celebrated its Tercentennial with a series of pageants, one of which reenacted repulse of the British at Scituate Lighthouse (built in 1811) by the Bates sisters, Abigail and Rebecca. One of the reenactors was Peggy Soule, S.H.S. class of 1937, with whom I first became acquainted in Indiana more than 60 years later! At Cudworth House, red-coated colonials were attacked by Indians, one of whom I spied crouching behind a bush smoking a cigarette! What a colossal disillusionment for an impressionable seven-year-old boy! At about this time, my father took me to the top of Mann Lot Road and showed me two ghostly brick chimneys, which were all that remained of a house named "Old Two Stacks." I shuddered to learn that the house was rumored to have had a whipping post in the attic, where recalcitrant

Scituate Lighthouse, 1950.

Old Two Stacks, Mann Lot Road, ca. 1900. Photo courtesy of Scituate Historical Society.

servants were supposedly punished. In fitting retribution, that unusual structure had burned to the ground some years earlier.

In the 1930's, every kid in Scituate knew the story of Thomas W. Lawson's rise to great wealth and subsequent fall to poverty. Dreamwold Hall was (and is) a continuing testimony to the opulence he brought to Egypt and Scituate Center. In front of his mansion stood a gigantic wooden flagpole that consisted, I believe, of only two pieces of Douglas Fir, and soared nearly a hundred feet into the sky. After Lawson's death, the pole was never repainted, but it survived into the 1950's before being cut down and removed. Alongside Lawson Road, which runs from Scituate Common to the former Egypt Station, there once stood a curious 2-story square building which had served as the judges' stand for Mr. Lawson's racetrack. Jack Litchfield and I often climbed the sagging staircase and gazed in wonder out the wide, open windows. As recently as the late 1930's the outline of the racetrack was still easily discernable, but hundreds of saplings foretold its imminent disappearance. This kind of wealth just could not be fathomed. In fact, Jack lived with his folks in one of the many gambrel-roofed houses that Lawson built in the Egypt area for various of his employees. Across the street from the judges' stand, not visible from the roadway, was an even more curious building – the beehive-shaped dovecote. This two-story cedar shingled structure was beautifully wainscoted, and had roosts for scores of pigeons. On one occasion, Jack and I loaded his wood-sided wagon with wainscoting boards from the second story, and trundled them to Jack's house. Then, realizing that this was stealing, even though the building was abandoned and deteriorating, we trundled all the wood back to the "pigeon coop" and reinstalled the wainscoting in its proper place. Another outbuilding had been a large decorative windmill, but all that Jack and I could find to mark its site was a number of interlocking rectangular chain links that survived a fire which had destroyed the structure some years earlier. During my schooldays, the same fate befell both judges' stand and dovecote – tragedies that may have been prevented had the preservation movement been more advanced. Years later, one of the former neighborhood boys admitted to a friend of mine these wanton acts of arson.

Shortly east of the former Egypt Post Office, across Lawson Road from the railroad tracks, there was during my boyhood a strangely flat, sparsely vegetated surface which had a blackened appearance and was covered with many thousands of rusty nails. I often walked this with Jack Litchfield, who explained that this marked the site of a huge barn wherein had been stabled the horses that ran on Tom Lawson's racetrack. At some much earlier time it, too, had burned to the ground. Carol Miles and John Galluzzo (2002) have compiled a fine story of Lawson and his estate that includes an image of this impressive structure, which was probably 200 feet long and perhaps 50 feet wide. Even as a charred outline this relic left an indelible impression on the mind of a young boy who collected, and then misplaced, a handful of those rusty nails as souvenirs of long-vanished wealth.

Most famous, of course, is Lawson Tower, which Tom built to hide the town's principal standpipe. This 153-foot-tall structure houses a lovely set of bells – "The Chimes" – which inspired the title of our high school yearbooks. For many years,

Lawson Tower, Scituate Center, MA, 1950.

starting no later than 1943, the cover of the *Chimes* was illustrated by an image of the tower that was designed by my sister, Marjorie. This cover was used until some years after I graduated (1946).

Sometimes, after school, I walked to the nearby home of a man named Billy Pepper to borrow the key to the tower. In those days, the tower was protected only by a padlock on the door, and one could gain admission simply by requesting the key. Access to the belfry is by means of a narrow spiral staircase, which lies inside a slender auxiliary tower attached to the much larger main structure. At the top of the stairs, one enters the belfry and can wander amongst the bells large and small – there are 10. From the belfry, my companion and I were afforded a stunning view of the ocean, which is just a mile to the northeast. Coming down the staircase was really a thrill, and not just a little scary. The stairs are so steep and narrow that a single misstep could send one tumbling all the way to the bottom. My biggest fear, however, was that someone would come to the tower and lock the door while we were aloft. Apparently, we never thought of taking the padlock with us, or locking it through the hasp before ascending the tower! Amazingly, the tower is sheathed in sawed cedar shingles, and requires re-shingling from time to time – surely at very great cost to the town, and in more recent times to the Scituate Historical Society. But what a prize attraction the tower was, and still is!

Since 1869, Country Way in North Scituate has been graced by the soaring spire of First Baptist Church – a large, two story wooden structure with cavernous second-story sanctuary and huge empty attic above. Presiding over this venerable institution, the Reverend Dr. Alan D. Creelman was kind, gentle, approachable by all and universally admired. He was a man of tremendous compassion and outstanding interpersonal skills, and loved to play ice hockey on Hunter's Pond with the North Scituate boys. As a teenager, ringing the tower bell for Sunday services often fell to me. The bell was so heavy that when it was swinging to an almost upside-down position, I'd be pulled right off my feet by the ascending rope. I had the immense pleasure of ringing that bell again during a visit to Scituate in the year 2000!

A large choir loft situated at the rear of the sanctuary concealed a little-known secret, for beneath that loft lay the long wooden ladder used to access the belfry and steeple. As relatively responsible members of a youth group, Christian Endeavor, and either then or soon-to-become members of the Church itself, Cobby Swift or Paul Miles and I felt no trepidation in asking Doc Creelman's permission to ascend the tower, and he

Rev. Dr. Alan D. "Doc" Creelman, 1959.

always generously produced the church key. After ascending the spiral staircase to the second floor, we pulled out that ladder and gently lifted it into position beneath the trap door by which one began ascent of the steeple. Above the trap door, we entered a much-darkened room containing the clockworks, which had long since ceased useful function, the clocks having been removed many years before. A short ladder led still higher, through another trap door into the belfry, whose huge bronze bell always received a sharp rap before we continued upward. A third ladder enabled us to climb into the tapered steeple, a very dark space cris-crossed by supporting boards that we used as steps to reach the top. At some time, pigeons had used the steeple as home, and the cross members were encrusted with their droppings. Whichever of us went first sent a shower of this stuff into the hair of the kid below. Near the top, we passed through a final trap door, giving access to a small floor, probably no more than 3 feet across, that is the highest point of the climb. There, at head height, and blocked by a small simple board shutter, was a tiny window from which we could gaze across the marshes and forested hills to bright blue waters of the Atlantic Ocean. Even in the slightest breeze we could sense gentle swaying of the steeple, causing us to marvel that the structure had survived essentially undamaged for nearly a century despite the frequency of northeast storms, an occasional hurricane, and even a direct hit by lightning!

## The Rianis

Once we had moved to 612 Country Way, we had new neighbors both across the street and on Hollett Street, down the hill behind our house. With the latter we connected immediately because Joseph and Lucy Riani, both immigrants from Italy, had daughters, Rose (Rosie) and Katherine (Katy), who were of babysitting age. A third daughter, Madeline, was

First Baptist Church, North Scituate, MA, 1980.

my age and became my earliest playmate and later a lifelong friend. Mrs. Riani's kitchen was always filled with tantalizing, delicious aromas of good food well prepared! From time to time, one of the older girls would come up the hill to our house bearing a huge platter of homemade spaghetti and meatballs, and what a delicious treat this was. Lucy hand rolled each strand of pasta, and reduced large blocks of parmesan cheese on a arched cheese grater fitted onto a wooden box containing a sliding drawer. Madeline still has the grater. As a frequent guest in that kitchen, I was treated to tasty slices cut from large round loaves of crusty Italian bread, and to small green crunchy peppers (probably pepperoncini), which were the first really spicy food I ever ate. A long narrow enclosed porch adjoined the kitchen, and it was there one day that Madeline and I were having a snack while sitting on small folding wooden chairs. Suddenly, my chair collapsed to the floor, squeezing my right ring finger with a scissor grip. My screaming brought Lucy running, and my bleeding finger was extracted and bandaged. The badly torn skin healed; the scar remains to this day!

Visiting our neighbor, ca. 1935. Left to right: Betty Hattin, Madeline Riani, the author, Marjorie Hattin. Photo courtesy of Madeline Riani Barry.

A player piano, the only one I ever saw as a boy, graced the Riani parlor, and it was a rare treat to sit on the stool, pump the pedals, watch the perforated roll move past, hear the beautiful music, and watch the keys move up and down as if by magic. Always coveting this instrument, I finally bought one for $50 at auction several decades later.[1]

Mr. Riani was a gardener by profession, and needed sharp tools to ply his trade. To this end he used a grinding wheel made of sandstone that was turned by means of a treadle and wetted by water dripping from a suspended, small-tipped tin funnel. He was kind enough to let a small boy sit at the wheel and pump the pedal, and this occurred often. Madeline still has the stone from that fascinating machine!

Mr. Riani had a small productive vegetable garden, but his family often purchased fresh vegetables from an open-sided produce truck which was driven house-to-house by Mr.

---

[1] Discovering that I could not even slightly budge the thing, and knowing that a hole would have to be cut in my family room floor to lower the piano to the basement, I talked to all the piano dealers in Bloomington, IN, and finally found one who would buy it from me for $40, and pick it up at the auction house. In the end, it was a $10 loss, which was more than compensated by the 24 hours of fun I had driving around town, talking to dealers, and eventually selling it.

Arthur Montanari. Arthur also sold fish, coal, charcoal and wood from that vehicle. On Saturdays, he was accompanied by a younger brother, Alfred, who was in my older sister's class.[2] Apparently, Arthur loved kids because he always had a smile and a wisecrack for us, gave us small pieces of ice to suck, and also gave us a few peas in the pod. Fresh from the pod, these were as much a treat as if he'd been handing out ice cream.

An essential ingredient in Lucy's cooking, mushrooms, came not from Arthur's traveling market but from woodlands which then dominated our town. These were a sturdy brown variety of mushroom with sponge-like underside that Mr. Riani cut into thin slices and dried in the sun on wide boards. This seemed a bit foreign, because no one in our own family had ever engaged in such a practice. After all, my mom had more than once recited to us a warning epitaph: "Here lies the body of Benjamin Bunny. He thought the mushrooms tasted funny."

---

[2]Alfred, Monty as he is known today, served with the Marine Corps during WWII. He was at the base of Mt. Suribachi on Iwo Jima when 6 members of his regiment, the 28th Marines, raised our flag at the summit and created a lasting symbol of American victories over the Japanese.

The Riani property boasted a tall, robust wild cherry tree which produced an abundance of not-very-sweet fruit. To enhance production, Mr. Riani and his nephew, Dominick, cut off the tree top, and attached to it with cloth and tar (?) several cuttings from a sweet-cherry tree. To my youthful amazement, these grafts, the first I had ever seen, took hold and produced the desired fruit! Another attempt to produce exotic fruit involved transplantation of a *fig tree* beside and close to the Riani barn. Each winter this tree was swaddled with insulation, and somehow survived the alien New England winters. As the tree matured, it did produce a few figs until one year, a year in which fig trees in Italy produced an especially high yield, the Riani tree mysteriously produced its own first bumper crop!

Upstairs in their barn, Mr. Riani had fitted out a simple apartment, this being occupied for some time by nephew Dominick (a great friend!) and Santi Strini. Santi was, like Mr. Riani, a gardener, and drove what even then seemed an *old* Model T Ford truck. Madeline and I enjoyed running to greet him upon his evening arrival, because he was amiable, was obviously fond of small children, and almost always had some interesting story to tell. His best story concerned his ears, or rather the absence of one ear. Where once had been a normal ear, there was now only a small hole. Santi told us, with no sense of shame or embarrassment, that as a young man he had lost that ear in a fight. Assuming that ears must be easy to lose, and not wanting to lose one of mine, I vowed then and there to stay out of fights!

Madeline and I began our formal education at Hatherly School, and our constant companionship waned as I came to know some of the boys in my class. To the consternation of some girls in our class, several of those boys developed a crush on a cute little pug-nosed blonde named Jean Mills. Determined that Jean should not steal undue amounts of attention, Madeline reacted with considerable ingenuity, and decided to duplicate "the Mills look." At night, using adhesive tape, she pulled up the tip of her nose, hoping for a change which she perceived would make her more attractive. Fortunately, her attempt at self-inflicted plastic surgery was a complete failure.

Today, Madeline remains my oldest and steadfast friend, and her nose is just the right shape!

## Cowboys and Indians

Playing cowboys and Indians was a favorite pastime during my childhood, just as it continues to be in many neighborhoods today. When I was eight years old, my parents outfitted me with a Tom Mix costume, complete with furry chaps, white "ten-gallon" hat, gunbelt, holster and pistol. My brother, Russell, got the Indian outfit, complete with fringed shirt, bow, arrows, and feathered headdress. It was as much fun to suit up as it was to actually play the game, but play at it we did until the novelty wore off.

The gunbelt, holster and pistol saw longer use, including a day in 1938 or 1939 when a group of us; including the Swift brothers, Gray Curtis, and others; wandered down Hollett Street, onto Ann Vinal Road, and then off to the right into a swampy area of soggy ground and tall hardwoods. There, the "gang" tied me to a tree, and relieved me of the gunbelt, holster and pistol, leaving me with only a lousy rubber dagger – a really

Playing cowboy (the author) and Indian (Russell) in our front yard, ca. 1937.

poor "trade." After they departed, I struggled against the ropes, finally broke free, and made my way home in a pretty dejected state. Mother, being pretty upset at the way I had been swindled, made a couple of fruitless phone calls. Alas, my trusty weapon and gunbelt were never retrieved! Today, the perpetrators of that youthful crime are among my oldest and truest friends, but I've often wondered what would have happened had the ropes held me more securely!

## Jere Ainslie's Store

Diagonally across the street from our home, and strategically situated with respect to Hatherly School, stood a small mercantile establishment operated by the venerable Jeremiah Ainslie and his daughter, Cecilia "Cecil" Brown. Outside the store, he was "Jere," but inside the store, he was Mr. Ainslie; however, despite her middle age, Cecil was always called Cecil.

The main attraction of Ainslie's was the glass-encased selection of honest-to-goodness *penny* candy – licorice cigars, red-tipped sugar cigarettes, Boston baked beans (red stingy things), mint juleps, the large-size gumdrops, caramel creams, walnettos, Tootsie Rolls, lollipops, and many others.

Another offering high on the list for those with 5¢ to spend was the popsicle, coming in root beer, grape, orange, lemon, and possibly a few other flavors. The thing that spurred us to buy a great many popsicles was a marketing tool known as the "free stick." One in every four or five popsicles produced a stick on which was imprinted with the word, "free." Such sticks could not be detected until that half of the popsicle had been consumed; the stick could then be presented to Jere, who dutifully produced the promised item! Necco wafers also cost 5¢. In addition to being thinner than those made today, they emitted a brief flash of light when taken into a dark room and broken in two. I broke a lot of them in dark rooms!

Another item of choice was soda pop, or "tonic" as it is called in that part of the world. Jere had three kinds of coke (we always used the full name), my favorite being Royal Crown Cola, the reason being that it came in much the largest bottle! We paid a 2¢ deposit on each bottle, and never failed to return ones that we had purchased or found on the roadside. Two cents was two cents! (Still is.) Finally, there were cupcakes, two to a package, with chocolate frosting. These, as with the candy, popsicles, and tonic, were just the thing to ensure tooth decay, and I ate *lots* of those cupcakes.

Jere was a taciturn man, who was usually found sitting in the "office" at the rear of the store. When one entered Ainslie's, a small electric bell buzzed and Jere would come forward to serve the customer, usually clearing his throat loudly so as to proclaim his approach. He showed remarkable patience with his young customers, who might take several minutes to select 5¢ worth of candy.

On one occasion, I asked Jere if he would save for me all the wooden cigar boxes as they became empty. He did so, and I soon had a number of them in use for my collections of "stuff." Jere had in the store a huge tomcat – the largest I have ever seen (or maybe I was just small). When I came in to collect cigar boxes, he would entice this cat onto a counter, don a pair of heavy gloves, and carry on a boxing match that was for real – the cat had not been declawed!

Jere once favored me with access to his photograph album, which included several images of Hatherly School made shortly after its construction in 1896. Small saplings lined the school driveway where, during my grade-school years, large beautiful maples had matured. It was Jere who informed me that so-called "Hatchet Rock" on the old Silas Pierce property is a corruption of the original name, which is Hatch's Rock. This made sense to me because the rock does not look like a hatchet, and there were plenty of folks named Hatch in the vicinity! Once standing boldly on the landscape, this gigantic glacial erratic afforded dandy climbing for young boys. Alas, development has eclipsed this amazing landmark, which is now crowded by houses, a large pine tree, and miscellaneous nondescript shrubbery!

At the close of 1945, Jere began to stock a large amount of surplus military gear – shirts, trousers, socks, navy sweaters, and even some backpacks and mess kits. I bought a pair of the wool U.S. Army trousers for about a dollar, and these became part of my Boy Scout uniform; I have them still, packed away in a basement trunk.

As for Cecil, she not only waited on store customers, but also gave piano lessons for 50¢ each. Lessons lasted an hour, and I took such lessons for about 6 months until pressing business (see "Construction Projects") became a greater passion. She was a kindly, soft-spoken lady who, like Jere, I considered a genuine friend.

Ah, Ainslie's Store. Where else for 10¢ could a kid completely fill one of those so-called 1/4 pound white paper bags with the kind of treats that were guaranteed to form cavities. Jere, Cecil and the building are gone, but the sweet memories and fillings remain!

*Tales of a New England Boyhood*

Hatch's Rock, latterly known as "Hatchet Rock," on Silas Pierce estate, ca. 1900. Photo courtesy of Scituate Historical Society.

## Mrs. Knowles and Pierce Memorial Library

Mr. And Mrs. Knowles lived off Country Way just a few doors from my home. He had been gassed during WWI and was rarely seen doing more than scything down their hay. Apparently his lungs had been severely damaged. She, however, was very much a lively part of North Scituate life in her role as librarian at Pierce Memorial Library. This imposing structure of stucco, stone and wood was approached by a semicircular drive which rarely contained more than one or two cars – most of us walked to the library. With stacks to the left and periodicals in a large semicircular area to the right, Mrs. Knowles occupied a centrally located desk, facing the main entrance. She was a mild-mannered bespectacled lady with white hair, a pleasant smile, and a wonderful way with children. The Scituate Town Report for 1946 lists Mrs. Knowles' salary as $532.50. Surely, her service to the community deserved a higher level of remuneration. From about the age of nine or ten onward, I was a regular patron, and spent many happy hours examining book titles and perusing the latest magazines. An all-time favorite of mine was a science fiction novel entitled *Two Miles Down*, about which I can now remember absolutely nothing. Except for those kept at the Swift home, I read all of the Tom Swift books. Cobby and Punch had checked out a few volumes of that series, and had then contracted scarlet fever. To prevent spread of the disease, the two boys were allowed to keep those books.

My favorite magazines included *Popular Mechanics, Popular Science, The National Geographic, The Illustrated London News,* and *Sailing* (or maybe it was *Sailboating*). In the last of these I often found myself scanning the "boats for sale" section, and once spotted an item advertising a schooner for a mere $200. I really wanted to buy that schooner! Of course, for that price the vessel was probably barely afloat, with rotting planking, leaking seams and bereft of rigging. Fortunately, $200 was not at hand, and the boat was in Maine, a combination which assured my exclusion from the yachting set.

Because of limited storage space, Mrs. Knowles could keep only a few months worth of each periodical, disposing of the older ones as new issues arrived. Happily for me, she saved back issues of *Popular Mechanics* and *The National Geographic*, and every few months would present me with a stack of these treasured magazines. From cover to cover, these were read with great enthusiasm, and discarded only after they had become dog-eared.

Mrs. Knowles passed away after I left Scituate, and that place of such wonderful memories has long since been converted to a private residence. Just think how much farther from home the kids of today have to walk or ride to find the sort of reading enjoyment that was inspired by our neighborhood library – the Pierce Memorial.

## Bicycles

My first and only bicycle was a Christmas present in 1940 – a Western Flyer balloon-tired model which cost the improbably low sum of $19.95. Bright red in color, it was a bare-bones model – no light, no bell, no carrying basket – but gradually, I added the necessary equipment. At last I had caught up with "Pete" Fleming (his real given names are Charles Frank); as a golf-club caddy he had earned enough to purchase his own bike a year or so earlier.  Further, his bike was equipped with a fluffy sheepskin seat cover, which made Pete's bike the Cadillac of its kind, and was the envy of most kids (well, at least me) in the neighborhood.  Tuning my bicycle became a regular pastime – tightening the spokes, lubricating the axles, taking apart and reassembling the coaster brake, and checking the tire pressure at Duffley's gas station in North Scituate Village.  Fiddling with the brakes produced no detectable improvement, and tightening the spokes caused substantial warping of the front wheel.

A year after my bike arrived, my brother received his.  This was also a Western Flyer, but cost only $17.95.  We often rode together, especially to North Scituate Village.  Riding without using the handlebars involved a balancing act mastered by nearly every kid in town, but on one occasion I carried this one step farther, and spread my arms sideways while passing George and Florence Fleming's house on Country Way.  I shouted back to Russell, who was behind me, "Don't try this," whereupon I heard a loud crash followed by shrieking and wailing of a seriously injured brother.  Hopping off my bike and running back to help him I discovered that his right forearm featured a strange kink.  Obviously, his arm was broken; while piloting two bicycles I walked him home.  Dr. Max Miles was summoned, and after the arm was splinted, Russell was taken

Russell performing a static test of his brand new Western Flyer bicycle, 1941.

to a Cohasset-based surgeon who set bones. Russell spent the next few days feeling pretty sorry for himself. He was only 10 years old at the time, so guess who got a dressing down for trying to keep him out of trouble?

## Satuit Playhouse

Weekend entertainment often included a visit to Satuit Playhouse, which I believe was a Paramount-owned theatre where first-run movies were often available. The theatre itself was quite lovely – all done up in a pretty elegant nautical style. Circular windows at the entrance simulated portholes, lobby floor and aisles were covered with Axminster-style carpets featuring a ropework design, and a simulated lighthouse adorned either side of the stage – one with a red light, the other with green. The nautical theme was carried out in costumes of the personnel, including that of Mr. Callahan (who tended the theatre door and deposited ticket stubs in an authentic brass binnacle) and the ushers – young women who wore navy-style slacks and blouses. These ushers used flashlights to guide patrons to their seats. All-in-all, this was a very stylish theatre the likes of which have pretty much vanished from the American scene.

The show started with Movietone News, was usually followed by a double feature, and included a cartoon. Saturday matinees had the added attraction of a serial feature, such as *Dick Tracy*, which required several week's attendance if one was to learn the outcome of the usually harrowing adventures. Price of admission was 10¢ for kids under the age of twelve, 25¢ for twelve and over. Being rather slight, I pushed my luck well beyond age twelve until the day Mr. Callahan swung his arm in front of me and asked how old I was. Learning that I was nearly thirteen he said, rather sternly, "25¢ from now on."

Of all the movies I saw as a child, a couple stand forth as particularly memorable. One, *The Octopus,* was supposed to be a comedy, but with blood dripping from what turned out to be a dummy hanging from the top of a lighthouse, an indelible impression of horror was left on my tender mind. Another was *The Wizard of Oz*. Of course, that film begins in black-and-white, but when Dorothy awakens in Oz the screen turns to color. Most of us, perhaps all, had never before seen a color movie, and there was an audible gasp and cries of "oooh!" from the audience. Most memorable of all was an event which occurred one Sunday afternoon on December 7, 1941, when a forgettable movie was suddenly stopped in mid-scene. The house manager strode onto the stage and announced that the Japanese had attacked Pearl Harbor. Showing of the movie was then resumed. All I could think was, "Where in the world is Pearl Harbor?" Alas, the playhouse is gone, and in its place are unseemly condominiums.

## A Military Convoy

Summer, 1942, found the nation fully mobilized for World War II, in which we had been engaged since the Japanese sneak attack at Pearl Harbor on December 7, 1941. One hot day we looked in amazement from our front yard onto Country Way, where a very long line of military vehicles had come to a standstill. This, we discovered, was a convoy which had originated at Camp Edwards on Cape Cod. Exactly why they stopped where they did, or why they stayed so long, never became clear, but presence of such an unusual phenomenon created quite a stir amongst the youthful populace. We hopped on bikes and rode towards the convoy's head, stopping in front of George and Florence Fleming's home to talk to the perplexed soldiers. Already, we had been purchasing defense stamps at school, ostensibly to buy jeeps, but we had only a vague idea regarding the size or character of that vehicle. Six soldiers were sitting in a relatively large 4-wheeled vehicle, and we asked if it was a jeep. They seemed puzzled, and admitted that as recent conscripts they weren't really sure. After acknowledging that their vehicle was probably a jeep, we then asked the name of the smaller, 4-passenger, 4-wheel-drive military vehicle which we knew to exist. That, they guessed, must be a "peep." Where they kidding us? Probably. That question aside, we were willing errand boys for the hungry soldiers, who gave us dimes and nickels for candy and cupcakes. Hoping that the convoy wouldn't move out, we raced our bikes to Jere Ainslie's store, purchased the requested goods, and raced back to the Fleming's house to deliver purchases shortly before the convoy once again began to roll. Small as it was, we had proudly made a contribution to the war effort.

## Curtis Home Bakery

During the 1930's and 1940's no visit to the home of my friend, Gray Curtis, was complete without a tour of Mr. and Mrs. Curtis' bakeshop. This structure, together with the Curtis home, a shed, and a small barn, stands on a large acreage off Ann Vinal Road that has been in the family continuously since 1646. One day in the mid-1930's, a friend named Bill Evans was at the Curtis home sampling a delectable homemade donut, and declared that if Mrs. Curtis would cook a few dozen he could sell them door-to-door around the town. Being a depression year the prospect of additional income was tempting,

Bakeshop of former Curtis Home Bakery, ca. 1986. Shed at right housed oil tank which fueled Glenwood stove used to prepare baked beans and brownbread. Photo courtesy of Gray Curtis.

so Eloise prepared the donuts, and Evans, confident that his scheme would work, drove off to test the market. Within three hours he was back, and told Eloise that he needed more donuts! Thus was born the Curtis Home Bakery. A bakeshop was set up in a small outbuilding and fitted with ovens, donut-making equipment, cooking utensils and other items essential to the baker's trade. Henry Duval was hired as night baker, specializing in bread, french pastries and cookies. Eloise Curtis baked and decorated birthday, wedding and other special cakes. Her husband, Bill Curtis, baked cookies, cakes and donuts. Bill Evans prepared pies, baked beans and brownbread; assisted the night baker; and made deliveries. Business burgeoned, a store was opened on Front Street, and Curtis Home Bakery became a Scituate landmark.

Whenever I visited the Curtis home to see my friend, Gray (Bill and Eloise's son), we invariably ended up in the bakeshop, where olfactory senses were all but overwhelmed by aromas of good things just out of the oven. What really caught my attention was the donut-making process. Bill Curtis squeezed donut dough from a cloth bag into a device which shaped the donuts, then lowered the device into a vat of hot cooking oil. When cooked on one side each floating donut was flipped over with a stick, and cooking proceeded until the second side was "done."

These donuts had a firm cake-like texture and a crispy light brown crust. As a confirmed and unrepentant donut eater I can state with authority that Curtis donuts, hot from the kettle, were surely among the finest, most delicious donuts ever cooked in the town of Scituate, and maybe in all of Massachusetts.

Loyal customers were aghast when, during the early days (1942) of World War II, shortages of sugar, flour, cooking oil, lard and even spices forced closure of Scituate's favorite bakery. Almost at once, Bill Curtis and Bill Evans enlisted in the U.S. Army, where each was commissioned a second lieutenant; Eloise and Henry Duval took jobs at the new Bethlehem Hingham Shipyard. Amongst regular bakery customers was none other than Boston's mayor, James Michael Curley, who had a weekend/summer home in Scituate. One evening in 1942, at a party hosted by Col. Philip Schuyler, the mayor was introduced to Eloise Curtis, who was also in attendance. Curley asked if she was connected to Curtis Home Bakery, and when she had made acknowledgment, said he was sorry about the closure and asked the reason. When Eloise had explained the problem, Mayor Curley declared that the bakery was needed as a good morale booster during the war. Asked if she could reopen the bakery, Eloise stated that this could be done if appropriate supplies became available. Curley turned to Col. Schuyler, who just happened to be head of the Scituate War Ration Board, and suggested that he make the necessary arrangements. Shortly thereafter, a large quantity of baking ingredients arrived at the Curtis home, together with a "C" gasoline ration card, which alloted considerable fuel for the delivery trucks. Henry Duval and Eloise quit their shipyard jobs, and with help from a few of Eloise's lady friends, reopened the bakery "for the duration." And, Mayor Curley was once again enabled to buy his treats![3]

## Auctions

While growing up in Scituate, I attended no less than four auctions, and was a cash-paying participant at the last of these. When I was only six years old, a neighbor named Ben Young passed away, and an auction was held to dispose of goods unneeded by his widow, Margaret. The actual bidding is beyond recollection, but I do remember Dad entering the high bid for an antique tool chest which was brimful of musty smelling old, even ancient, tools. Among the more interesting items were a nickel-

---

[3] When WWII ended, the original bakery staff was reassembled and Curtis Home Bakery flourished until final closure in 1968. Much of the original equipment is still in the building which served so well as a bakeshop.

plated .38-caliber revolver, a large and handsomely fashioned Indian axe head, and a hand-operated device for pulling teeth.

My second auction experience took place on Branch Street, nearly across the road from the office of Dr. Grovestein (Grovey, as he was widely known). By this time (ca. 1936) I understood what was going on, but had no money for purchases, and didn't know exactly how to bid or what to bid on anyway. Two items only linger in my memory – a matched pair of flintlock pistols. One of these had a crackled grip and sold for $5.00; the other, seeming in my eyes to be in very fine condition, sold for $6.00. I often wish that it had been possible to buy the latter, the only such antique I have ever seen at auction.

A third auction experience occurred in 1938, when goods of neighbor William Burton were put up for sale. Again, only a single item comes to mind – the game of Camelot, which even now may be available in stores. The auctioned set, comprising playing pieces and instructions, lacked the game board. My sister, Marjorie, bought these items for 50¢, and constructed a suitable board based on a figure in the instruction pamphlet. Happy memories of playing that game, which is similar to but much simpler than chess, induced me to purchase Camelot for our own children and grandchildren.

By the time of a fourth auction, I was a "seasoned veteran" of such an event, which included items donated to the First Baptist Church for a fund raiser. Prices were very low, so the field full of goods could not have yielded much more than a few hundred dollars, but the reader must remember that this was in the early 1940's. Among the items was a seltzer bottle and box of $CO_2$ cartridges. Pretty steamy items for a Baptist affair, but these sold quickly. My first purchase was a large wooden pipe which had been salvaged from the sanctuary when a modern Hammond organ was purchased. The fate of that pipe, for which I paid a quarter, is recounted in the chapter "Construction Projects." I also bought a large, round pedestal-type oak dining room table and four chairs. At the time, oak furniture was a drug on the market, and I got the entire outfit for 40¢. A plan was formulating in my mind to build a stage at ground-floor level on one side of our barn, and put on plays. This brainstorm got as far as cleaning up that side of the barn and installing a light socket on the ceiling. We never staged a play, but one has to concede that such an idea had considerable merit. When Dad sold our Country Way home in 1948, the table and chairs were a bonus for the buyer.

## Private Property

In the carefree days of my youth, walking across private property – fields, woods, swamps or marshes – was a commonplace practice, and owners, if they ever did see us, never shooed us off. In all my wanderings, I never saw even one "no trespassing" sign.

I particularly remember a holly tree which was growing in a woodsy area off the west side of Mann Lot Road, more or less across from the home of scout troop committeeman Louis Haartz. Apparently, existence of that tree was common knowledge, and by the age of thirteen or fourteen I made annual trips there to cut off a few small branches for Christmas decorations. One had to hike a couple hundred feet off the road to reach the tree, passing a very small pond en route. The owner of that property remained a mystery to me, and besides, holly trees seemed not to be uncommon in the area. Only later did I discover that Scituate is just about the northern limit of wild holly, which extends into Massachusetts only along a narrow strip of land close to the sea.

Pine trees abounded in an area of North Scituate which lies southwest of State Highway 3A and just north of a gravel quarry known as "the pit." In two successive years, just before

Christmas, I walked the mile and a half from my home to the pit, dragging my sled all the way. Beyond the pit was a wood known as "the pine forest," followed by the "T-field" – so named because of its shape. Crossing a fence at the far edge of the T-field brought me into Mr. Wheelwright's pasture, his property being situated in the town of Cohasset. There, scattered across the landscape, were many shapely white pine trees from among which I selected a particularly fine specimen. Tying it to my sled I then trudged homeward, pretty much chilled to the bone. Going out into the woods to cut a Christmas tree was a fairly common practice, and if landowners had any objection they never showed it by erecting "no trespassing" signs. Most likely, they never realized that any of the trees had been taken. How very much different the situation is today, with signs and fences long emplaced almost everywhere, and landowners usually becoming more than a little put out by presence of trespassers!

## Seavern's Store

North Scituate Village had several attractions of interest to a young boy. Litchfield's Farm Market stood beside Country Way, just up the hill from the village itself. Presided over by an affable man named "Joe," this was the place for fruits and vegetables, in season. Lying at the foot of the hill was Seavern's Store, a true general store featuring foodstuffs, dry goods, and hardware. A tall, slender man named Franklin Sharp managed the first of these, Edith Agnew the second. But it was Alonzo "Lonnie" Pratt, in charge of hardware, who attracted all of my attention. It was here that I purchased nails for all of my building projects, and it was Lonnie who taught me the difference between 6 penny, 8 penny, and 10 penny nails. Much later, I learned that these denominations refer to the colonial period cost of 100 nails of respective sizes. Obviously, the larger nails cost more. Here, too, I bought one of those neat hay rakes which have wooden teeth made from dowels. This rake was needed to gather up hay from our back field that was I cutting with Dad's scythe by age twelve. Enviously, I eyed the lengths of manila rope which came up through the floor from basement reels, but bought only sisal because it was cheaper. Lonnie was a great favorite of mine – always patient, always asking about my current project. Each year, he marched in the Memorial Day parades with a group having the name "The Sons of Veterans". The age of these gentlemen suggested that most were sons of veterans of the Civil War, bringing to mind that the war had taken place not so very long before.

*Donald E. Hattin*

# Haircuts

Fabello's North Scituate barber shop occupied a corner of the Bailey block, and sported the familiar rotating red, white and blue symbol of his trade. During the 'thirties, haircuts were 25¢, regardless of whether he trimmed remaining fringes on the head of a balding man or the unruly mop on that of a lad long overdue for tonsorial attention. Based on boyhood photographs, I was clearly in the latter group. I always had a comb, but rarely

Building in North Scituate Village (aka "The Corners") which housed Tony Traniello's "Sunny Spa" and Fabello's barber shop (arrow), ca. 1931. Photo courtesy of Scituate Historical Society.

used it, and my mother often joked about "twitchets," those unruly hairs which stood straight up off the rear of my head.

Three unchanging features characterized Fabello's shop, these being the smell of hair tonic (Wild Root was one of them), a pinball machine, and radio broadcasts of baseball games. Radio stations received news of ongoing games by telegraph, the announcer monotonously reporting progress after translating incoming Morse code signals. First, one heard a long series of dots and dashes, then the announcer would say, for example, "Ball one." Another series of clicks, and he'd say, "Strike one." This was colossally dull, and probably accounts for my lifelong disinterest in the sport. Pinball games cost 5¢, but having only the quarter entrusted to my care, I did not play. One day, however, Mr. Fabello handed me three fake coins and said, "These are slugs. Play the machine." Surely, he thought I'd get hooked, but his ploy failed.

One day in 1945, while working at the A&P store, I decided to join ranks with the growing number of boys who sported brush cuts (= butch haircut), but thought such a style was called a "whiffle." Store manager Jim Ward granted permission for me to take a half hour off so that I could visit Fabello's shop. There, I asked for a "whiffle," little realizing what was in store for me, and Mr. Fabello proceeded to cut all hair on the top of my head to a length of about one inch. When done, he waxed that hair, then combed it upright. Whereas this style may have been popular during the roaring 'twenties, it would make me a laughing stock in the 'forties. I had the appearance of someone who had been frightened nearly to death. I paid my 50¢ (haircuts were by then more expensive than in the 1930's), left the shop, hopped on my bike and peddled furiously homeward. There, I quickly shampooed my hair to remove the wax, applied a generous amount of hair oil, and slicked my hair down so as to mask its shortness. Back in the store no one could have guessed all that had transpired during the past 45 minutes!

Another memorable haircutting event took place later in 1945, when I was still determined to have a brush cut. Alden James, a brush-cutted classmate, learned of this desire and concocted a scheme which would be mutually beneficial. He had electric hair clippers and needed a trim; I had long nondescript hair that required a complete overhaul. Alden convinced me that we could each cut the other's hair, and thus save money. On the agreed upon day, we met at his home, and I carefully manipulated the shears so as to give him a very decent trim. Then he went to work on me, with predictably horrible results. My hair is very fine, and would not stand up. Furthermore, Alden's brush-cutting skill should have been reserved for cutting brush!

With a now very short and raggedy haircut, I looked exactly like a rain-drenched monkey. Slicking the hair down to hide the ugliness didn't work. There was not enough hair left to slick.

## Really Bad Windstorms

One of the deadliest storms in New England history occurred during fall, 1938. Without the sophisticated weather warnings of modern times, a hurricane of tremendous force and violence struck an area extending from southern Connecticut to well north of Boston, and dozens of communities suffered immense damage. Newspapers were filled with photos of smashed houses, stranded vessels, autos crushed by fallen trees, steeples toppled, flooded towns, derailed trains, displaced tracks and collapsed bridges. In Scituate, coastal damage was considerable, downed trees lay everywhere, and electric power was out for many days. Town crews used axes and hand-operated saws to clear the streets, and it was several days before traffic could flow unobstructed. Schools were closed until buses could run and power was restored. As a nine-year-old, I had little appreciation of the wide-ranging extent or horrendous damage that had been done. Of the five hurricanes I have experienced, four of them seriously affecting Scituate, the storm of 1938 was by far the worst, and has left an unerasible memory of nature's occasional rampages.

Over the years, northeast storms – nor'easters – have wreaked more total havoc on Scituate than all the hurricanes combined. Along the shore, seawalls have been hammered to pieces, rebuilt, and broken again; cottages lining the shores have been shattered and rebuilt, only to be shattered again; and flooding of low lying areas has caused no small amount of hardship for those whose homes were left isolated by waters many feet deep. I recall a mid-1930's northeaster during which a rescue boat was launched from Bailey's Causeway into the adjacent, deeply inundated salt marsh to aid families which had been marooned. Quite alarming to me was a fierce storm of the mid-1940's, when winds were tearing branches off trees in our yard, and perhaps even toppling a few in the neighborhood. I decided to investigate. Slipping quietly out of the house and into the tempest, I started walking down the middle of Country Way. Power had failed, and in the blackness just beyond Hatherly School grounds, I found myself ankle deep in unseen water. The entire roadway was flooded. For an instant, a burst of lightning revealed a most frightening sight. Power and telephone lines had snapped, and some sagged to the ground near the very spot where I stood. By that time, my feet felt the unmistakable buzz of electrical current. I was in great danger of being electrocuted! What to do? Immediate retreat was imperative, but which way? I chose to get off the road, and quickly. Two great leaps brought me to the sidewalk, from which I ran into Mr. Whiting's yard and over to the schoolyard fence, which was a chain-link affair. With both hands on the top rail, I vaulted the fence in synchrony with a tremendous flash of lightning and almost simultaneous crash of thunder. For one desperate moment, I had a vision of fried Donald, but luck was with me. In whole or in part, this adventure never, repeat never, invited an encore.

## Electric Carts

Two of our near neighbors were Mr. and Mrs. Edward Coverly Newcomb, who just happened to be parents of Cobby and Punch Swift's mother. Everyone knew that Mr. Newcomb was a brilliant man who had invented numerous devices connected with motive power – efficient diesel carburetors, two-cycle engines, and many more. Sometime in the mid-1940's, perhaps motivated by gas rationing, Mr. Newcomb designed a three-wheeled electric cart powered by an automobile battery, featuring a single front wheel steered by a tiller-like lever, and large enough to carry an adult. His plans were conveyed to a local craftsman, Mr. Litchfield, who had a wonderful array of hand tools in the Bayfield Shop on Country Way, North Scituate. Mr. Litchfield went to work on the cart, producing a truly handsome vehicle, which was coated with glossy green paint. Mr. Newcomb, dressed in a suit and looking quite aristocratic, piloted this splendid vehicle along Country Way, where every kid in the neighborhood watched with considerable awe and no small amount of envy.

The practicality of this electric cart was not lost on Ross Schultz, proprietor of a North Scituate fuel-oil company, and he set out to build one for himself. Quite soon, his son David (for unknown reasons, he was known as "Chupey") could be seen driving the Schultz electric cart along Country Way, and one evening when Chupey drove the cart to Hatherly School, several of us just had to have a look. Schultz's machine was built on the same principle as Mr. Newcomb's, differing only in refinement. All three wheels were taken from balloon-tired bicycles, and the front fork of a bicycle held the single front wheel. Electricity was furnished by a 6-volt automobile battery, which powered an automobile starter motor and chain drive that turned a sprocket on the rear axle. Speed was controlled according to the number of coils (hand made using heavy gauge copper wire) through which the electricity flowed, a long-handled screwdriver serving as a rheostatic control lever. When our curiosity had been satisfied, Chupey told us that the battery was low, but suggested we lean against the front and try to keep the cart from moving. We couldn't!

## Climbing a Standpipe

Off the upper end of Mann Lot Road, North Scituate, the town water department constructed a large standpipe in order to furnish pressure for much of the area's water system. A steel ladder rose to the top of that tank, and offered a huge challenge to certain teen-age boys. Not only was the tank impressively tall, but the lowest ladder rung was something like 12 feet above ground level. Paul "P" Miles and I decided that climbing the standpipe was an absolute necessity; therefore, armed with a 100-foot length of 3/4" manila rope that I had purchased through the Sears Roebuck catalog, we biked to the site and got to work. First, we tied a rock to one end of the rope, then tossed the rock toward the lower rungs. After a few tries, we succeeded in looping the rope over the second or third rung, then tied the up and down lengths together. With feet braced against the tank, first one then the other, we climbed the rope hand-over-hand up to the base of the ladder. Of course, we hauled the rope up behind us so as to ensure its presence on our descent. Next came the dizzying vertical climb to the top, thence onto the "roof" of the standpipe. What a view! The Atlantic Ocean lay before us, a sparkling bright blue expanse in the brilliant afternoon sun. We lingered no more than 10 minutes before descending. The challenge had been met, the splendid view was a bonus!

## Steam Trains

When I was a boy, steam-powered trains were the norm on tracks of the New York, New Haven & Hartford Railroad, which bisected Scituate. From about the age of five until I was ten or eleven years old, the sound of an engine whistle found me scurrying to a high spot in our back yard so that I could watch the train chugging rapidly across the salt marsh east of Hollett Street. That stretch of track sported a semaphore signal, which descended to horizontal position as a train passed. Minutes later, the semaphore arm rose to a 45° position, and eventually rose back to vertical. Usually, I watched until the action stopped, long after the train had vanished. Dual tracks permitted the passage of several trains per day in each direction, trains being so commonplace that amongst the hundreds of photographs in our family albums not one depicts a railroad scene!

As I and my friends grew older, we daringly placed small metal objects on the rails, and delighted in the flattened results

*Tales of a New England Boyhood*

following passage of a train. Nails were reshaped to look like the letter "T," and pennies changed from round to oval. Knowing the possibility of derailment deterred us from trying larger objects, although the idea of flattening bolts had crossed my mind a time or two.

Once, while walking beside the tracks with Cobby Swift, we spied a couple walking towards North Scituate *between* the rails! The wind was against them, and they did not hear a rapidly approaching train. We yelled as loudly as possible, and upon hearing us, the approaching train, or both, the couple leaped aside, the man to one side and the woman to the other. Realizing the separation, the man leaped back across the track, narrowly avoiding being struck by the engine. Not so lucky was a Cape Verdean (then called a Portagee) named Manuel _____. When I worked in the North Scituate A&P store, Manuel came in every evening after work and bought a kraft-paper shopping bag (2¢) and a package of Granger smoking tobacco. The purpose of his shopping bag was obscure, but he always walked home (towards Egypt, MA) along the railroad tracks, and may have used the bag to collect lumps of coal, which commonly fell off the train's tender. One day, as a few of us were fooling around on the Swift family front porch, a steam train passed by and suddenly came to an unscheduled stop a couple hundred feet beyond the Swift home. Punch Swift decided to investigate, and several minutes later came back with an ashen look on his face. Manuel, who we later learned had epilepsy, had apparently collapsed on one of the rails, and the engine had cut his body in two. A tragic end to a friendly old man.

At North Scituate, as elsewhere along the railroad, each workday ended with arrival of a train from Boston at about 6 p.m., and large (it seemed to me) numbers of businessmen and a few women descended to the platform. During summertime, many of the older men wore flat-topped straw hats ("boaters") which were in fashion into the mid-1940's. From the baggage

Steam-powered train approaching North Scituate railroad station during a snowstorm, ca. 1930. Photo courtesy of Scituate Historical Society.

car came bundles of newspapers, which were scooped up by young fellows who were paid for delivery to the newsstands, notably the "Sunny Spa" operated by Tony Traniello. Some of the passengers had picked up papers in Boston, others bought them in North Scituate – for 3¢!

A final anecdote of steam-train history is recounted in the chapter entitled "Ben Meyers' Farm."

## Forest Fires

It was common knowledge that sparks from a steam locomotive could start fires along the right of way. Putting out these blazes was achieved by use of the Fire Department's Model A Ford truck, a few hundred gallons of water, and the many volunteers who showed up to use back-mounted, hand-operated water sprayers. When the blaze had been extinguished, one of the firemen wrote down names of volunteers, and each eventually received a check for services rendered – about 75¢ per hour. These payments were duly recorded in the annual Town Report. Volunteers learned fire locations by listening to the number of blasts on air horns, these being situated at several locations around town. My service usually took place in fields and marshland in the area between North Scituate station and the Hollett St. crossing. Such fires were fairly frequent, leading to popular belief that some of them were set by means other than locomotives, thus furnishing an exciting way to earn some spare change. The largest fire in which I participated occurred on Bulrush Farm, the blazes requiring several hours to extinguish. I put out one blaze which was advancing along a 200- to 300-foot front. My dad, who had come over from the nearby Whiting Milk plant on Gannett Road, leaned on a broom for at least three hours, and along with me was listed in the 1944 Scituate Town Report under the heading "Forest Fires." Each of us was paid $2.25!

## Winchester .22 Special

Grandpa Hattin's gun collection included an octagon-barrel, pump-action Winchester repeating rifle which used .22-caliber ammunition called "Remington special." My dad inherited this weapon, and for years it hung on a wall in our home. No one ever told me how to fire a gun or, for that matter, ever told me not to. Naturally, a day came when I just had to find out what that gun could do. Target practice in a sand pit situated close to the Mann Lot Road standpipe was a good place to find out. So, taking a few cartridges (Kleenbore brand) from a high shelf in our pantry, I loaded the rifle and headed on foot to the pit. If any Scituate law restricted teen-age kids from carrying a loaded rifle, such law was certainly unknown to me. Anyway, it was in that pit that I learned to cock and fire a rifle. A bit later, I bicycled to the town dump on Stockbridge Road, where rats were known to live in abundance. Surely, no one would object to the disposal of rats by a highly experienced marksman! Now, the Remington .22-special cartridge is considerably longer than a .22-caliber long rifle cartridge, and has a larger diameter such that the .22 special will not fit in the chamber of a standard .22. Further, the effect is *much* more powerful. When shooting with buddies, we learned that a rat hit with a .22 short will wiggle a bit, then die; a rat hit with a .22 long will die instantly. When hit by a slug from my .22 special, the dead rat was flung back 2 or 3 feet!

My final shooting trip to the dump was with Elden Meyers, who on that occasion drove us there in one of his dad's farm trucks. While in the process of dispatching several rats, we noticed some kids playing near a substantial and neatly stacked pile of newspapers. These had been salvaged from the trash with intent to sell. Suddenly, the kids started yelling, and we saw that the newspapers were aflame – big time. A truck driven by a very angry looking man came jouncing down the potholed lane. Stopping near the blaze, he questioned the kids, and they pointed accusing fingers in our direction. Elden and I hollered that we had not set the fire, hopped into the truck, and sped off. Whether or not the angry man believed us, we did *not* set that fire!

## Pa Swift and His Pool

Something of interest was sure to take place during a visit to the Swift home, which was situated between the First Baptist Church and tracks of the NY, NH, & H Railroad. For several years, neighborhood kids gathered there each Wednesday evening to join Mr. Swift while he listened to his favorite radio program, *The Lone Ranger*. From first notes of the *William Tell Overture* to final echoes of "Hi Ho Silver, Awaaaay," each of us listened with rapt attention. "Pa," as we called him, demanded absolute silence throughout the show, and backed up this expectation by laying a .45-caliber six shooter on the arm of his comfortable Morris chair. Another activity involved a board game called Bonanza, which we usually played on Swift's front porch. This game featured a green felt playing surface and poker chips. Pa Swift presided as rake-wielding croupier, wore a green gambler-type visor, and laid his pistol on the table to ensure the absence of cheating. I wonder what "Doc" Creelman thought when he strolled up one evening and found a number of his youthful charges "up to their ears" in gambling!

Cobby and Punch Swift had a modest sized rock-and-mortar backyard pool used for splashing around and sailing their boats, including a fairly large tin ocean liner which moved by means of a nifty wind-up motor and steel propeller. One day in 1942, these fellow Boy Scouts and great pals of mine decided they needed a bigger pool, and grabbing some tools began to dig. Pa Swift immediately got involved, and soon a huge hole had been dug – a pit about 12 feet wide, 25 feet long and perhaps 8 feet deep at the deepest end. Encountering some large glacial boulders, they hired a truck-mounted derrick and removed all but the largest of these obstacles. Using scrap pipe and baling wire, Pa directed construction of a reinforcement framework, then the building of forms using scrap lumber. At that time, the Bethlehem Steel Company was creating a new shipyard in nearby Hingham, MA, where large amounts of concrete were being poured. Each evening, excess mix had to be dumped from the mixing trucks. By knowing the right people, Pa arranged to have some surplus concrete mix "discarded" into the space between the wooden forms of the nascent swimming pool. Using long sticks of wood, several of us tamped the mix so as to eliminate possible bubbles in the finished walls. A pipe was laid to the creek which flowed at the downslope edge of Swift's property, and a wheezy old electric pump was installed to convey water to the pool. This had to be done at low tide, because the creek became brackish at high tide. A homemade ladder and diving board at the deep end completed the job, and the filled pool became a regular gathering place for the neighborhood boys, and also girls when we started dating. At one point, Pa announced that all of us would have pool privileges during his lifetime. He lived up to that promise. The pool had no filtration system, but was regularly treated with chlorine, and drained and scrubbed on a monthly basis. Once, after scrubbing down the pool walls, Pa ordered the water turned on. Strangely, water from the inlet pipe flowed steadily, even though the wheezy old pump normally produced a pulsing flow. Just then, a member of the water board "happened" by, and Pa told one of the boys to turn off the wheezing pump. The switch was flipped two or three times, and the influx of water stopped, but not before I noticed one of my friends reaching armpit deep into a slender hole. He was turning off the valve of a hidden pipeline which tapped the town water supply. If the board member suspected this, he politely declined to say so. Late in life, Pa Swift was named Citizen of the Year by the Town of Scituate!

Four pals standing in front of Swift's swimming pool, 1945.
Right to left : Punch Swift, the author, Cobby Swift, "P" Miles.
Photo by Louis Haartz, courtesy of Ward Cobb Swift.

## The *Rainy Day*

Boy Scout committeeman Louis Haartz was a great favorite amongst troop members living in his neighborhood. He kept us laughing at his somewhat off-color jokes, and proved himself not only a versatile craftsman but also a very careless one. Sometime in the early 1940's, Louie decided to build a sloop, and proceeded to fabricate it in his side yard. Much of the wood came from local forests, especially the white cedar destined to become planking for the hull. The boat was to be 30 feet in length and was given the name *Rainy Day*, apparently alluding to some distant date of completion. For a keel, Louie fashioned a huge oaken timber into which he hand chiseled mortises designed to receive the ribs. Oak was also used for the ribs, most of which would have a sort of S-shaped configuration. To produce these ribs, Louie heated water to boiling with a wood fire beneath a long trough-like pan. Once heated to the boiling point, each of the ribs-to-be was bent to the proper shape by placing one end then the other into the crotch of a nearby tree, and applying the necessary amount of muscle power. Bottom ends of each rib were then fitted into appropriate mortises in the keel and fastened with galvanized nails, the boat slowly taking on the graceful lines shown in plans that Louie himself had drawn. Planking for this vessel was to be made of white cedar derived from trees cut in a local swamp. Using only a band saw, Louie shaped each piece, and fastened them to the ribs with brass screws. There was only one problem with all of this. Louie had the unfortunate habit of sweeping wood scraps from the band-saw table, and from time to time, lost a finger joint to the moving blade. By the time the hull had been completely planked and the deck beams were in place, Louie had lost a majority of the finger joints on his right hand and even part of the thumb. Eventually, he gave up, and the partly finished boat was sold. For a time, it reposed in the side yard of a house situated at the corner of Curtis Street and Country Way. Later, it was to be seen behind the barn of the Eddie O'Donnell place in Marshfield, where it lay still unfinished for several years. At least for Louie Haartz, the rainy day never came.

# Chapter 12
## Apples, Sea Moss, And Other Odd Jobs

Pretty early in life, many kids find numerous ways to earn spending money because there is so much on which to spend it. The first jobs I had were connected to my weekly "allowance," that word being a euphemism for "low hourly wage." Our yard was divided into several plots, separated from one another by our driveway, the front walk, and a hedge. All mowing was done with a heavy, cast-iron reel-type mower the use of which netted me 25¢ per week starting at about age eleven. By age twelve, I was also entrusted with the job of filling the 5-gallon glass bottle which fueled two of the six burners on our hybrid kitchen stove. Four of the burners burned natural gas, the other two having oil burners beneath round cast-iron lids such as were featured in old-fashioned wood-burning stoves. The latter part of the stove was kept hot winter and summer, even on the hottest days. As my dad got more involved in his work and became less interested in the yard, I also pruned the privet hedges that separated the front yard from the rear of our property. The hedges totaled at least 200 feet in length, but despite the extra work, my allowance never exceeded 25¢.

Across the street from us lived Ben Young's elderly widow, Margaret, who had built a small house on her property so that she could live simply and rent the larger house. Her new house had a small sitting room, small bedroom, and small kitchen where water was supplied to her sink by a pitcher pump. She cooked on a cast-iron wood-fired stove. Often, when the mood or my mother prompted, I collected, cut and split a few armloads of wood and delivered it free of charge to Mrs. Young. Supplies of wood came from a scrap pile behind our barn that

Mrs. Ben Young and neighborhood kids, ca. 1940. Left to right: Russell Hattin, Marjorie Hattin, David Ward, the author, Johnnie Savage, Mrs. Young, Lyn Savage.

derived from repair jobs occasionally carried out on our buildings. Some of the wood came from fallen branches of the many trees that dotted our property. Margaret was a kindly soul, and always good to any children she happened to meet. She raised and sold houseplants, and once gave me a small potted cactus which I nurtured for several years before heading off to college. Mrs. Young lived well into her nineties.

Late one summer, probably in 1939 or 1940, the Bailey Company of North Scituate needed some help distributing handbills to the homes of summer residents who were heading back to the city. Mary Bailey drove us through several neighborhoods, and two or three of us youngsters placed the handbills, actually like postcards, on the doors of homes on First, Second and Third Cliffs, and elsewhere along the shore. The handbill started out with the words "Going Home?" and was followed by a note about Bailey's availability to winterize plumbing systems. This job was really fun, and we earned 10¢ per hour. Not bad for kids only ten or eleven years old.

At about this time I became, for a mercifully short few days, a magazine salesman. While walking along the Country Way sidewalk, I was approached by a man who had been driving along looking for likely lads to peddle magazines door-to-door. For each sold magazine, the pay would be 5¢. This sounded like a good deal, so I agreed to take a cloth sack filled with magazines – *Liberty* was one of them – sell the magazines, and meet the fellow at this same spot in a week's time to turn in my receipts. Well, selling magazines during the closing days of the Great Depression was not easy, and sales that week totaled only seven items. A week of toting that heavy bag for 35¢ was inducement enough for me to end forever my days as a magazine salesboy.

During the fall of 1940, when I was eleven years old, I joined a large number of grade-school, junior-high and high-school kids in the interesting job of picking apples for Mr. Ralph Brown. He operated a large orchard on Bulrush Farm, which was situated off Hollett Street on Battles Hill. I started picking at 10¢ per hour, but immediately learned that kids in junior high onward were earning 25¢ per hour, and my wage was quickly corrected to the latter sum. We picked apples via the expedient of a three-legged step ladder that could be nestled deeply into the trees. Each of us picked into a small burlap sack slung over the shoulder by means of a 2-inch-wide strap. When the sack was filled, the picker would call "Hee Lee" in a long, drawn-out fashion, and an English girl named Brian Healy came to collect the sack and hand up an empty one. Full sacks were emptied into square pine bushel boxes, and eventually these were taken to the Bulrush Farm apple stand on State Highway 3-A near the Scituate-Cohasset town line. For several days, I believed the pickers were calling out "Tea Leaf," and so followed suit. Noone noticed my naive error. Brian may have been one of the many British children who were sent to America during the Nazi bombings of southern England.

No part of the orchard was more fun than that which contained Baldwin apple trees. These ripened late in the season, and some were so large that hardly more than a dozen would fill the picking sack. A few of these apples were almost too large to be picked up by one hand, and were 5 inches or more in diameter. Bulrush Farm exists today only as a neighborhood of homes built where lush orchards of apple trees once held sway – pity. Apple picking was fun, lots of fun, with friendly kids, plenty of apples to eat, and crisp autumn air – one of the most enjoyable odd jobs a young boy could hope to land.

At age twelve, other than our own yard, I also mowed lawns for a few neighbors, most notably for the Shine family, who lived for a time in a house on Country Way opposite the junction with Studley Royal Road. The usual fee was two bits! A particularly interesting job came my way when an older single lady named Belva Merritt, who lived diagonally across Country Way from Hatherly School, asked if I would like to clean up her shed. The building was actually an enclosed shop, and contained an amazing variety of items left behind when her father died. She told me to take anything I could use, and put the rest out for disposal. Among the items thrown away were dozens of pigeon nests, each comprising a pressed composition bowl mounted on a small square wooden base. A tangle of tools, nails, bolts, cans, bottles and other junk was discarded, but I did save the head of a shingling hatchet and several cartons of brightly colored calcimine. Later, I mixed these pigments with water, and painted parts of our interior barn walls some gaudy blue, purple and orange colors. My interest in tools and building things led to construction of a small workbench along one barn wall, using an extra set of slats that had come with a recently purchased bed. It was there that I converted the shingling hatchet into a functional tool. Not knowing that a wooden handle could have been purchased at Seavern's Store for a few cents, I flattened one end of a short length of ¾" pipe and rammed this into the hatchet head. The resulting tool was not only very dull, but also unreliable owing to the fact that the head was not aligned properly. Ultimately, this shortcoming was cause of a severe wound to the thumb of a friend, Ducky Chipman, whose one attempt to use the hatchet was a complete misfire.

When I was thirteen years old, a newcomer to town, Mrs. Frank Drewitt of Captain Pierce Road, inquired at Jere Ainslie's store about her need for a young boy to do general yard work that would not include any heavy lifting. Jere recommended me for the job, for which payment was to be the princely sum of 35¢ per hour. For much of summer, 1941, I worked several hours a week doing general cleanup, raking, weeding and gardening to help refurbish a yard which had been much neglected by the previous owner. I do remember one Saturday when I worked five hours at the Drewitts, and earned $1.75 – my highest daily wage up to that time. This job ended abruptly after a several-week stint because I had the temerity to speak up about having to push heavy wheelbarrow loads of dirt that were supposedly not to be included in my duties.

Just before the outbreak of World War II, Scituate was the sea-mossing capital of New England. Sea moss, or Irish moss as it is commonly called, grows on rocks and ledges below the low tide mark and is a variety of brown marine algae that develops a bushy form as much as 4 to 6 inches tall. When sun cured and pulverized, the moss was used as a gelatin in food processing. Freshly collected moss was brought to one of the mossing beaches, which were simply parts of a beach that were used for drying and curing the freshly harvested algae. Young men, usually in their late teens and early twenties, collected the moss and sold it to one of the mossing-beach proprietors. Typically, the mossing boat was a dory of the kind used by Gloucester fishermen. Narrow at each end, and with a beam much wider than the bottom, these boats handled very well in rough water and could hold several hundred pounds of wet moss. Moss was raked from submerged rocky ledges by means of a mossing rake, which had an extremely long handle (11 ft. or more) and closely spaced, sharp-pointed, wedge-shaped teeth. Our local blacksmith, "Teke" Sherman (William Tecumseh Sherman), made nearly all of these rakes. Mossing was best done at low tide, when a number of mossers could be seen in action along rocky parts of our coastline. As the tide rose, or as soon as the dory was full, the mosser would head for shore and sell his harvest at a rate of 2¢ per pound, wet. A platform scale was used to weigh the moss, and the moss was paid for in cash.

Mossing beaches were tended by other young men, and occasionally girls, who spread the wet moss across the sand. Within a day, the moss dried out and turned more or less black in color. The moss was then wetted and turned frequently, gradually bleaching to a very pale yellowish color. This "cured" moss was next pitchforked into large square gunny sacks and stamped down so as to make the heaviest possible bale. I can picture vividly the stamping process – young men attired only in bathing trunks doing a sort of "mossing dance," shifting their weight first to the left foot for two hops, then to right for two more hops. Thus, the cured moss was packed tightly into the bales, which were approximately a yard square and 4 or 5 feet long. When full, the bale was stitched shut with a large needle and baling twine.

At that time, as a youngster of only twelve years, I had neither the size, inclination, nor money to become an offshore moss collector. What I did do was wait for the exceptionally low tides that for two or three days each month accompany a full moon, and wade out and hand pick moss in areas where the water was too shallow for the mossing boats. There, attached to cobbles and boulders that could not be raked because of their small size and curvature, the previously untouched moss had grown to unusual luxuriance, and I could easily fill two or three standard burlap potato sacks within an hour. One of the hazards of this occupation was the occurrence of tall, sharp-shelled barnacles (genus *Balanus*) on some of the rocks where the moss was collected. These cut deep gashes in my feet, the cuts taking all summer to heal because I was so frequently in the water, but the money made the pain worthwhile. I would never have dreamed of wearing my sneakers while in the water.

Usually, I had only one pair of summer shoes, and the idea of getting them wet or cut up by barnacles was unthinkable. My companion in this enterprise was Joey Bonomi, a neighbor with whom I palled around for several years. Together, we transported our harvest, around 80 to 120 pounds of wet moss each, to the nearest mossing beach, which was actually a man-made "beach" situated at the edge of a former farm field more than a mile from the shore. The moss was so heavy and the bags so ungainly that we had to "walk" our heavily laden bicycles the entire distance. Our pay, anything from $1.60 to $2.40 for a couple hours work, was very high relative to earnings during the recently ended depression. Even in 1942, kids my age could earn no more than 25¢ or 35¢ per hour for odd jobs, so the sums we earned while mossing seemed pretty awesome. So, for three or maybe four days each month, we made the ritual trip to North Scituate Beach at low tide, and spent happy moments bending down, sometimes completely submerging our heads, to collect this strangely valuable product of the sea. We never realized that lower-than-normal tides also occur during the dark of the moon, and thus missed many golden opportunities to amass even greater fortunes!

Once, determined to get a larger price for my hard-won harvest of moss, I decided to cure the stuff at home and then sell it for the 21¢ or 22¢ price that was paid for the cured product. To do this, I had to build a large wooden platform in our back field, and lay out the moss to dry. I let rain and dew substitute for hose sprinklings, and eventually turned out what I thought was fully cured moss. My brother, Russell, was a partner in this venture, although he had not collected nearly as much moss as I. Dad drove us to Scituate Harbor, where we delivered our gunny sacks of dried moss to Dwyer's mossing beach. Dwyer inspected the moss, pronounced it to be black and white (partially cured) and allowed us 12¢ per pound. In the end, fast handling and improper weighing of our sacks enabled Russell to get just about as much money as I did. Because of the large weight loss during drying, and all the work involved in curing, plus the effort required to deliver the moss to Dwyer's, I decided that selling the wet moss for 2¢ per pound was the only profitable path. Thereafter, we sold our moss wet.

A few years ago (in the 1970's or early 1980's) an article in *Yankee Magazine* featured then-active Scituate sea mossers. Some of these were described as professional men who had shrugged off the double-parked acquisitive life to return to work they had enjoyed as young boys – raking sea moss from rocks along the coast, using boats equipped with outboard motors instead of the oars which had been standard during their youth.

Interestingly, the price of wet moss had risen only slightly since those earlier years.

There comes to mind one final "odd job," which was carried out in the company of my pal, Pete Fleming. Mr. Whittemore, stepfather of one of our high school classmates, had taken over management of the Scituate Country Club, the fairways of which were in poor shape because of disuse during World War II. Under the supervision of Jerry Cahir, who was pulling several reel-type mowers with a neat little Worthington truck, we raked up matted grass all day, with a short break for lunch (furnished). This tall grass was later burned. At day's end, Mr. Whittemore paid Pete and me $5 apiece, which was a fairly handsome sum considering the times and pleasant nature of the work.

But let us backtrack just a bit, to 1943. That was a banner year financially because in the spring, at age fourteen, I began a fine experience as stock boy and clerk at the North Scituate A&P Store, the story of which is in Chapter 14.

# Chapter 13
## Scouting Adventures

During the fall in which I reached the age of twelve, classmate Bob Holcomb asked me if I would like to join the Boy Scouts. Without a moment's hesitation I said, "Yes," and embarked on an ardent membership that was to occupy much of my free time for the next five and one-half years. On the very next Monday evening, I attended the regular weekly meeting, which was held in the gymnasium of Scituate High School.

The author, wearing his brand new Boy Scout uniform, 1941. Note campaign hat, scout handbook in right hand, and official Boy Scout jackknife on belt.

Our weekly scout meetings were conducted in part by the scoutmaster, at first Fred Dorr and then Bob Cowdrey, and in part by the junior assistant scoutmasters, including, in order of service, Bill Ayer, Matt Miles, and Punch Swift. Each of these 5 leaders had a strongly positive effect on troop development, and each of those who came under their wise and skillful leadership has much for which to be grateful.

During the first meeting I attended, junior assistant scoutmaster Bill Ayer asked me to choose which patrol I'd like to

Troop 5, Scituate, MA, 1943. Left to right, front row: Punch Swift, Fred Dorr; second row: Bobby Fernandez, Hugh Frasier (sp?), Eddie Veiga, Russell Hattin, Manuel Spinola, Bob Rich, Bob Sternfelt, Jimmie Robinson. Author in back row, between flags. Photo by Louis Haartz, courtesy of Ward Cobb Swift.

join. Many of my closest friends were members of the Cuckoo Patrol, headed by Matt, the older son of local physician, Dr. Max D. Miles, so that was the patrol I selected. Matt proved to have excellent leadership qualities and quickly had all of the younger scouts working on requirements for the tenderfoot badge. Again and again he urged us to "know our stuff," and learn it we did. I especially remember instruction in first aid, which has served me well on many occasions, most especially that in which one of my college students fell during a field trip and broke both bones in her lower leg. I splinted the leg before we carried her nearly a mile along a railroad track to an ambulance summoned by two runners who had been sent ahead to call for assistance. As in any good scout troop, all requirements were to be satisfied fully, such that the first-class 12-mile hike requirement meant 12 miles, not 11½! Matt was a perfectionist, and the younger scouts profited greatly from his example. On a pace-and-compass map involving a roughly triangular traverse of some 1½ to 2 miles, Matt's error of closure was about a quarter inch. My map of a similar though rectangular area, drawn to the same scale, had a closure error of an inch.

The very first weekend of my membership found our troop engaged in one of the long hikes which mark the scouting experience. We met in that part of town known as West End, at the home of the Holland family. Teddy Holland led us on the hike, following woodland trails, traversing stretches of secondary roadway, and culminating at the summit of a tall hill which afforded a spectacular view of Hingham Harbor. Upon returning to our starting point, Bill Ayer explained that we would end the day by visiting a not-too-distant site, known as the Mill Pond, which had been made available for troop use by the Scituate Water Department. There, the ancient earthen dam and spillway were found to be intact, but the millrace and gates had long since disappeared. In their place was a pile of logs, brush and other debris that sufficed to retain only a small volume of water. With bare hands, we began to remove this debris so that the small pond could be drained and the foundation built for a new set of gates. A week or so later, when this job was completed, we actually uncovered some of the sill timbers from the original grist mill. Although I could not envision it at the time, various activities at the Mill Pond were to occupy much of my time for more than five years! Under the expert guidance of troop committee chairman Ward "Pa" Swift and his colleague Louis Haartz, and with the mechanical assistance of a stripped-down Model A Ford that had a homemade dump body, we hauled sand, cement, rock, and logs to the site, and within a year had erected a masonry dam and supporting log-and-earth cribwork.

*Tales of a New England Boyhood*

The new sluiceway was fitted with 2"x12" planks which could be used to control the level of impounded water, and by this means we created a sizeable body of water. Here, then, was the means to meet the swimming, rafting, canoeing, and skating needs of an entire generation of Troop 5 scouts as well as the corresponding age-group of girl scouts.

In those early days of Troop 5, Matt went by the nickname "Bugs," which was in no way meant to be derogatory. His younger brother, Paul, later known simply as "P," was also in the Cuckoo Patrol and is to this day a faithful friend. For our patrol campsite at the Mill Pond, Matt selected a level spot just

Model A Ford "truck" at Mill Pond dam site. Left to right: Pa Swift, Sarge Bartlett, Punch Swift, Cobby Swift, Matt Miles. Photo, ca. 1942, by Louis Haartz, courtesy of Ward Cobb Swift.

Mill Pond, after dam and several cabins had been erected. Photo, ca. 1944, by Louis Haartz, courtesy of Ward Cobb Swift.

landward of a shoreline ledge of granite, and there we built a three-sided Adirondack-type shelter. Built by hand of pine logs, and thatched with pine boughs, this shelter accommodated four boys sleeping side by side. Our fireplace was situated in front of the shelter, close to the granite ledge, and we spent many a happy evening cooking our meals there and enjoying the special kind of camaraderie which can be captured perhaps only once or twice in a lifetime.

During my years as a scout, I made steady progress through the ranks from Tenderfoot to Eagle. At about the time I was a Star Scout, I became leader of the new Buzzard Patrol, with Don "Skinzo" Waite as assistant patrol leader. A principal ac-

*Tales of a New England Boyhood*

Adirondack shelter constructed at the Mill Pond by members of the Cuckoo Patrol. Photo, ca. 1944, by Louis Haartz, courtesy of Ward Cobb Swift.

complishment of our patrol activity was selection of a campsite and construction of a patrol cabin. A great windstorm had occurred early in the 1940's, and produced a "blowdown" of pine trees about a quarter mile away, and it was there that we selected logs which were to be used in our cabin. In a single weekend, patrol members cut, trimmed and hauled enough logs to complete the basic structure. While the logs were being cut to specified lengths, I notched their ends in the classical manner with a hatchet, and fitted them into place. A door was fashioned on one end, and log rafters were erected to support the roof. The roof and gable ends were made of used lumber, which was hauled to the Mill Pond in a horse-drawn wagon driven by patrol member Donald Ford. For reasons I will never understand, the finished cabin measured only 5' wide and 6' long. In the right-rear corner, we installed a small, cast-iron potbellied stove, and vented this through the wall via an uninsulated stovepipe. Along the left wall, we built two bunk beds. The upper was fine for me at 5'10", but Skinzo was at least 6 feet tall and had to sleep in a somewhat cramped position. The attic was tiny, but could accommodate three of the smaller scouts. To guard against attic entrapment, gable-end boards were just barely tacked onto the frame, so even a nudge or gentle kick would allow for quick escape. Skinzo and I spent many happy nights in our little log cabin, with Bob Rich, Bob Sternfelt, and Jimmie Robinson usually in the attic. Those three made us laugh to the point of weeping with their nightly rendition of the new "Chiquita Banana" radio advertising song. Once, when the fire in our stove had diminished to glowing coals, I tossed in a few small logs, then added a little boy-scout water (kerosene). The heated fumes exploded and sent the cast-iron stove lid crashing up against the ceiling. Fortunately, no one was hurt, but we learned another of life's lessons – the hard way as usual. Alas, our cabin did not stand for long. After I had gone off to college, the troop leaders decided that structures containing anything other than natural materials would be taken down, so our little cabin was sawed into four pieces and destroyed!

During the winter of 1940/41, patrol meetings were followed by jousting matches using stout quarter staffs that were kept in a special locked closet where other meeting materials were stored. These staffs were grasped with hands spread wide apart, the attacker hitting first left, then right, then up, then down, and the defender positioning his quarter staff to ward off each blow. Lots of fun, and no one got seriously hurt. With the onset of WWII, however, our main physical activity became marching, which was carried on indoors or outdoors depending upon the weather. I loved the discipline that marching required, and enjoyed immensely the patriotic parades which took place each Memorial Day. No longer was I an onlooker at Groveland Cemetery in North Scituate, eager to scramble for spent shell casings following the legionnaires' salute to departed comrades. Now, proudly and in full scout uniform, I became part of these grand parades. Parading was carried out at each of the town's many cemeteries, beginning, I believe, at Mt. Hope Cemetery in the West End. School buses carried the marchers to and from each cemetery, and the parade formed along the adjoining road at some distance from the graveyard entrance. Many civic, fraternal, veterans, and military-related organizations took part, including Veterans of Foreign Wars, American Legion, Sons of Veterans (of the Civil and probably also Spanish-American wars), Women's Auxiliary (of what I can't recall), Red Cross, Boy Scouts, Girl Scouts, for a time the Sea Scouts, the Town Band, and perhaps some other groups. The parade was headed by flagbearers followed by the Scituate Town Band, which played martial airs and was led by a splendidly attired drum major who held a gleaming baton and wore a tall black busby. As the column entered a cemetery, the music stopped, to be replaced by a solemn drum roll punctuated by the muffled beat of a bass drum. When all were in the graveyard, including spectators, the boy and girl scouts assisted in placing a new U.S. flag on each veteran's grave. A brief prayer was followed by three salutes from a squad of riflemen equipped with WWI Springfields. After the ceremony, we formed up, marched back to the buses, and traveled to the next cemetery (Groveland), where the whole process was repeated. I often wonder to what extent these patriotic traditions are carried on today.

Almost as soon as the war broke out, the government issued an urgent call for various kinds of scrap – aluminum, rubber, iron and steel, paper, and cardboard. Throughout the conflict, Troop 5 was engaged in various scrap drives, beginning with aluminum, which was in extremely short supply. This was a

*Tales of a New England Boyhood*

Part of commemorative parade at Scituate Common, ca. 1940.
Dad is third from left in nearest column of legionnaires.

door-to-door activity because almost no one had enough aluminum to create a roadside pile. Nearly everyone gave something, and I remember receiving from one elderly lady a very fine aluminum water dipper which surely would have served well for all her remaining years. I hasten to point out that in 1942 many Scituate homeowners continued to rely on hand-dug wells for household water, and some of that water was still being drawn up by hand.

Second among the scrap drives was a huge one to collect iron, steel, and assorted other metals such as copper and brass. Local contractors furnished trucks, many of which were driven by volunteers, prominent amongst whom was Mr. Samuelson, our high school band and orchestra teacher. From all points in town, scrap was picked up from piles in people's front yards, and the filled vehicles were taken to a scrapyard in Braintree or Quincy. There, scrap piled up so fast that it couldn't be handled, so we had to pile the scrap temporarily in a field adjacent to the Fitts grain mill in Greenbush. Some scouts took advantage of this drive by cobbing a few choice items – a shotgun in one instance, and a brass alto (or baritone) horn, later pawned for $5, in another! Boys will be boys – but scouts?

Our longest drive was for scrap paper and cardboard, which was generated continuously by consumers, and which we collected until war's end. Periodically, we gathered paper and cardboard from around town and took it to an unused bay of Charlie Lane's Egypt Garage. We bundled cardboard and magazines, and baled the newspapers using a hand-operated wooden baling device. For this kind of scrap we received some remuneration, and near war's end had accumulated several hundred dollars for purchase of raw materials that the troop used to build a wonderful log cabin at the Mill Pond. Logs for this building were obtained in Marshfield at Hatch's Mill, one of the last, if not *the* last, water-powered sawmills in Massachusetts. The resulting well-built structure measured approximately 16 by 22 feet, had a covered porch and log-shuttered windows, and inside had a cast-iron woodstove at one end and a stone fireplace at the other. Our cabin was the scene of many outings for both boy scouts and girl scouts, but within a dozen or so years had been burned to the ground by heartless arsonists.

World War II resulted in an extended period of rationing, which especially included gasoline, shoes, meat, butter, canned goods, sugar, and bicycles. Tires? Well, the ones we had had to last because there were to be few replacements "for the duration." The war also brought about a mammoth civil defense effort that affected everyone in town. We were aware of concrete coastal observation towers which were built in the Glades, but we did not know of the local antiaircraft gun battery there until after the war. We did, however, hear the coastal defense

Troop 5 cabin at the Mill Pond that was built with money earned during scrap paper drive. Author standing on porch, 1946. Photo furnished by Ward Cobb Swift.

Scoutmaster Bob Cowdrey (in cab) bringing a load of scouts and their gear back to First Baptist Church after camping at the Mill Pond, ca. 1946. Note front left tire of Bob's Model A Ford coupe. Photo furnished by Ward Cobb Swift.

guns being practice fired at the entrance to Boston Harbor, and watched the numerous Navy blimps ceaselessly patrolling the shore in their search for never-far-off German submarines. My father was among the many volunteer airplane spotters who stood at coastal watch sites and called in configuration, altitude, and flight direction of every plane that traversed the coastline. His spotter's guide, which depicts silhouettes of all kinds of allied and axis warplanes, resides in my library to this day. For the duration, all homeowners were required to fit windows with dark green or black pull shades so that the entire town could be blacked out during an actual or practice air raid. All of the boy scouts received extensive training in first aid, including use of tourniquets and traction splints. The latter were fashioned by our local blacksmith, William T. "Teke" Sherman. Several

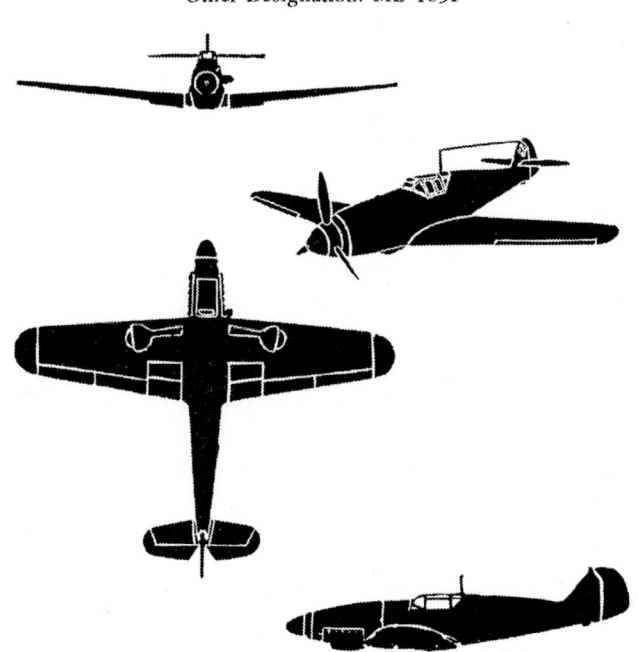

Page from Identification of Aircraft spotter's guide issued to members of the Army Air Forces Ground Observer Corps, for which Dad was a volunteer. Manual is dated 1942. (While visiting East Germany in 1985, the author met a fellow geologist, Kurt Ruckholz, who had piloted an ME-109F during WWII.)

scouts were organized into an emergency patrol, each member building a practical two-wheeled first-aid cart rigged for towing behind the scout's bicycle. Other scouts, including me, received a white Civil Defense armband on which was embroidered a gold lightning bolt on a circular field of blue. This armband signified that we were couriers, whose job it would be to carry emergency messages in the event of power outages during a bombing attack. We were assigned in pairs to various command posts around town, each staffed by us and two or more air-raid wardens, and we were activated at the sounding of air-raid sirens. These warnings were signaled by air horns at each of the town's fire stations. Normal use of these horns was for signaling, by number and spacing of blasts, the locations of a fire. At the special air-raid signal, we scouts would hop on our bicycles and ride quickly to our designated posts, mine being at Greenbush fire station, about 2½ miles from home. All traffic was supposed to cease within twenty minutes of the air-raid signal. My partner was Sarge Bartlett, who lived on Booth Hill Road a mile or more from my home. When an air-raid signal sounded, and it almost always came conveniently at about 7:00 p.m., after everyone had finished dinner, Sarge hopped on his bike and pedaled like mad to my house, from which we proceeded pell-mell to the fire house. We always managed to get there within the alloted 20 minutes! To take a message anywhere in town necessitated knowledge of the entire road system, including names of more than a hundred streets, roads, avenues, lanes, etc. We took our responsibilities seriously because the German threat along the east coast was very real.

Among the more humorous episodes of our Civil Defense activity was participation in a motor ambulance corps drill which enabled the lady volunteers to practice their newly learned first-aid skills. Scouts were enlisted to serve as "victims," and were spotted at various locations around town. Each of us wore a large label indicating the kind of injury to be dealt with. A dispatcher gave each group of volunteers a list of "victims," and the ladies drove their beachwagons (aka station wagons) to assigned sites to administer the necessary treatment and furnish transport. I was labeled "broken forearm," but by the time the arm had been splinted and supported by a sling, it surely would have been broken in a couple more places. After assisting me into their vehicle, the ladies drove to the next site, where the victim was labeled "dead." This injury apparently exceeded anything in the dear ladies' training, so they hoisted the "body" into the station wagon and pulled out a heating pad, activated it by adding water, and placed the pad on the victim to keep him warm. We scouts nearly choked in an effort to stifle our laughter.

During fall, 1944, a young girl named McGrath was reported missing from the Harbor area of our town. She was about thirteen years of age, reported to be very attractive, and suspected of being the victim of foul play. Many search parties were organized, including one that involved a number of scouts from Troop 5. On a glorious Sunday afternoon we climbed aboard the Swift family's 1931 Buick beachwagon, affectionately known to all as "the jeep," and with "Ma" Swift at the wheel proceeded on a search that commenced in the Greenbush area and from there followed the entire length of Old Oaken Bucket Road. We searched in a swath extending a few yards on either side of the road, eventually reaching the crossroad known as Sherman Corner. Turning left, we searched the roadside as far as the Norwell town line, then searched along other roads in the Scituate part of the area. I recall that the girl's body was found in a wooded area on the Norwell side of the line, just a few hundred feet from where our searching had stopped! Towards five o'clock, Ma picked up the scouts and drove back to the Swift home, this being situated behind the First Baptist Church. In the church, a youth group known as "Christian Endeavor" was about to start its weekly meeting, and several of the boys invited me to come in. I declined, out of shyness rather than religious indifference, and turned to walk home. Four of

*Tales of a New England Boyhood*

Swift family's 1931 Buick beachwagon, known as "the jeep." This vehicle delivered 9 miles to the gallon of gasoline. Photo, ca. 1945, was furnished by Ward Cobb Swift.

the boys, including Cobby "Twit" Swift and Sarge Bartlett, grabbed me by the arms and legs, hauled me into the meeting room, and dropped me in the middle of the U-shaped arrangement of benches on which youth-group members were seated. With somewhat wounded pride, I got up, took a seat on one of the benches, and looked across to the opposite side. There, staring at me as if I was a scarecrow, sat the most beautiful girl I had ever seen. She was Marjorie Macy, the girl in the wet picture from "P" Miles' wallet. There is definitely such a thing as love at first sight, because it happened to me then and there. That lovely girl was destined to become my wife!

Just once in my scouting career, during the summer of 1945, I attended Boy Scout camp. That summer, when our troop went to Camp Child, in Plymouth, MA, I took time off from my job at the A&P store, and joined in two weeks of continuous learning, camp work, and just plain fun! As in previous years, our troop was assigned to Camp White, which was one of several camps named after men who had been influential in establishing the facility. These smaller camps were scattered along the shore of a fine pond called Morey's Hole, at one end of which was a large dining hall commanded by a hefty cook named "Dutch." Because of our arrival time, one of the first activities was dinner in this hall. Each troop occupied its own long table, and was served by the boys who sat at the table ends. These scouts scurried to and from the serving area to fetch large pans full of food. Evening meals were tasty, filling, and fun, usually ending with a round of songs such as the following:

> I stuck my head in the little skunk's hole
> and the little skunk said, "Well bless my soul,
> take it out, take it out, take it out, please remove it."
> Well, I didn't take it out and the little skunk said,
> "You'd better take it out or you'll wish you had,
> take it out, take it out, phssssst," I removed it.

These songs were terribly corny, and we knew it, but everyone joined in the fun and all of us had a merry time.

**Breakfast was also served at the dining hall,** but lunch was something else. Just before noon, a couple of designated scouts from each camp hurried to the dining hall to pick up so-called "hot boxes." These metal containers held the makings of our midday meal, whether hot, cold or mixed. The beverage was invariably a Kool-Aid type of drink that we called "bug juice." Bread, peanut butter, jam, and a piece of fruit were staples, and cold cuts were often included. Occasionally, something bizarre showed up in the hot box, such as a two-foot-long codfish together with other ingredients and instructions for preparing fish chowder. On that occasion, Camp White scouts made a considered decision, dug a hole, and gave the poor fish an honorable burial. Peanut butter and jam tasted better than usual that day!

Most boys chose a daily activity which would earn credits toward one of the scouting ranks or merit badges. I selected canoeing, which turned out to be a fine choice. We had a great instructor named Sykes, who really knew his stuff and made canoeing a great deal of fun. We started out by learning standard paddle strokes, including the J-stroke for the aft paddler, the cross-bow rudder for the forward paddler, etc. Once these strokes were mastered, each of us was required to swamp a canoe out in deep water and then empty it and climb back in. This was done by pushing the stern of the swamped canoe downward under water until the canoe stood nearly vertical. Then, by shoving the stern upward, the canoe would shoot up out of the water and come to rest about three fourths empty. Next, one rocked the canoe up and down from the stern end, waited until remaining water was sloshing forward, then pulled his body up over the stern and slithered down into the canoe, hopefully before all the water came sloshing back to again submerge the stern! Once inside, the canoeist splashed out the last water by hand. All of this took quite a bit of skill, and we prided ourselves on being able to master the technique. Another thing Sykes taught us was the art of gun'l jumping. For this exercise, the canoeist stands on the gun'ls back toward the stern. Then, by alternately crouching down and standing up, the canoe is propelled forward with a series of slapping sounds as the bow alternately rises above and then comes down onto the water. Using this technique, a canoeist can easily outdistance a rowboat with two oarsmen.

Toward the end of our camping experience we learned how to paddle a really large "war" canoe that held about 10 or 12 paddlers, whose strokes were controlled by a steersman called the coxswain (cocks'n). Our troop raced against another troop for the full length of Morey's Hole. The call to stop was a split second too late, and before we could bring the heavy craft to a halt we slammed bow first into the dining hall dock, thus knocking down everyone in the canoe. We all laughed heartily at that mishap, and no one was hurt.

Occasionally, our day's activity included a hike, and there was a day when several boys in my troop hiked to a fire tower that was situated not far from the pond. From the top, I could see a scout camp that was at the opposite end of Morey's Hole from the dining hall, and it was obvious that several scouts were active near the waterfront. I let out a loud yell, catching their attention even at that distance, which must have been over half a mile. Then I began to use semaphore signals to see if anyone there could read such a message. I signaled, "Don Hattin" and got a response, "Elmer Walster". Elmer was well known around Camp Child and was one of the leaders of his troop. Neat!

On another occasion, our troop picked up lunch fixings shortly after breakfast and headed out along a trail that led ultimately to an ocean beach at Ellisville, several miles south of Plymouth. There, we spent much of the day clowning in the water and on the sand. One of the day's highlights was burying all but the head of one boy, Bobby Snow, I believe, and just the head of his brother, Tom. With the two lying side by side, and with Tom's hand stretched out to hold Bobby's chin, it appeared that just one person was involved, that person having removed his head and placed it a couple feet away.

Camp White offered many opportunities for improvement, and it was exciting to start projects for that purpose. During the first week I built a Y-shaped dock, using scrap lumber and basing the whole thing around a couple of small pilings that must have been part of an earlier dock. Another project involved cutting down a dead pine, stripping its bark and setting up the trunk as a flagpole. Then, I shinnied up with a bucket of paint and painted the pole from the top downward. It is hard to imagine why I didn't paint the pole before I set it up. Still another project involved lining the approach paths with rounded cobbles, which gave our camp a neat appearance. For these and other projects, I was initiated, toward the end of camp, into the "Order of Doog Gnituocs." The ceremony took place at night, and ended with presentation of a string neck loop on which was hung a small cloth bag. Into this, each of the counselors placed a small object that represented one of the qualities each Doog was to manifest throughout life. Each of the initiates was instructed never to open the sack to see the contents. As insurance against overpowering curiosity, I soon stitched the bag shut; I still have that little bag, but have not yet peeked inside. The contents *feel* like small rounded pebbles about the size of corn kernels.

When camp sadly drew to an end, we piled into Bill Appleton's school bus for the 30-mile ride home. For me, it was a happy time because during camp I had received first-ever letters from my girlfriend, Margie Macy, and going home meant seeing her after what seemed an interminably long absence.

Just after Christmas, 1945, when gasoline was no longer rationed, two of our troop committeemen, Pa Swift and Louie Haartz, organized a wonderful trip to the White Mountains of New Hampshire. To prepare for this trip, I bought a pair of very heavy woolen trousers which itched so badly that I considered wearing flannel pajamas beneath them. Late in the evening before our departure, my dad stopped by Sidney Gates' clothing store in North Scituate and bought me a much more suitable pair of long johns. Heavy woolen socks and rubber-bottomed "barker boots" insured warm feet. Layers of shirts and a good parka, plus a red plaid woodsman's cap and warm gloves completed the necessary attire. Each of us took along a sleeping bag, because our quarters were to be quite primitive. Pa and Louie had arranged with Joe Dodge, well-known proprietor of the Appalachian Mountain Club Lodge in Pinkham Notch, for us to stay in a bunkhouse adjacent to the lodge, and for us to take meals at the lodge. The bunkhouse was spartan, but adequate, and was heated by a wood-burning stove consisting of a 55-gallon oil drum turned on its side. Of course, we kept the stove well-stoked during daylight and evening hours, but by morning the bunkhouse was frigid! Each night, we talked ourselves to sleep, recounting each day's activity, and for some reason laughing uproariously when Gray Curtis repeated at intervals, and in a falsetto voice, the word "Bab-O." Someone got the fire going each morning, and we had no sooner dressed than the call to breakfast was heard. Someone at the lodge sounded meal call by swinging a piece of pipe between two yard-long lengths of railroad rail, these being suspended by leather thongs from a crossbeam outside the lodge. This call was repeated at lunch and dinnertime, all meals being included in the small cost that each of us was charged.

During the day, we variously hiked up the snow-bound trail to Tuckerman Ravine, an amazingly steep-sided glacial cirque, or practiced our tobogganing and snowshoeing skills on slopes closer to the lodge. Our stay was only for two or three nights, but the experience etched itself indelibly in my mind because of the sheer wonder of the environment, our enjoyment of winter sports, the camaraderie and humor of the bunkhouse, and wholesome food at the lodge. All of us were impressed by, not to say envious of, Cobby and Punch Swift, each of whom had received as Christmas gifts that year a briar pipe and tin of Prince Albert tobacco. It would be three more years before I commenced pipe smoking, which I then continued for thirty eight years!

Cobby Swift, "P" Miles and I were close friends all through our schooldays, and remain so to this day. After each of us reached the rank of First Class Scout, we proceeded to earn the merit badges which would lead to Star, Life and Eagle ranks. The merit-badge counselors were selected according to their special skills, and expected solid performance on all requirements. I well remember taking my specimen of cedar-shingled plywood to Mr. Richard Brown for part of the carpentry requirements, and my samples of soldering to Mr. Evan Bailey for part of the metal-working badge. For the cooking merit badge, I prepared a full meal over an open fire for Pa and Ma Swift. The entreé was swordfish, but it wasn't until the meal was finished that I learned about their general dislike of fish. Even so, both enjoyed my culinary efforts. Some merit badges were required of all scouts, others were elective. The toughest was civics, which required detailed knowledge of all aspects of federal, local and county governments. Earning this merit badge required reading, telephone calls, interviews, and attending a court session in the town of Hingham. Because a principal industry was truck gardening, one badge required listing the kinds of equipment in use on each of several local farms. It was then that I learned, from Mr. Prescott Damon, the nature and use of a lump masher, which consisted of a series of 2"x10"x4' planks nailed together in imbricate fashion and drawn by a horse or tractor to break up clumps of soil in a newly plowed field.

During our senior year in high school (1945-1946), three of us, Cobby, "P", and I completed all requirements for the rank of Eagle Scout. Together with parents, we drove to Hingham for the investiture ceremony, where each of the several new Eagles was introduced to a large audience and presented with a beautiful Eagle badge. Each of us was also given a small Eagle badge, which was then pinned to the dress of the individual scout's mother. My mother wore that pin to her grave less than a year later. The impressive ceremony in Hingham was followed by a local one sponsored by the Scituate Kiwanis Club. Police Chief Michael Stewart, club president at that time, presented each of four new Eagles with a walnut-mounted metal plaque on which were engraved the words "Eagle Scout Recognition," and also presented each of us with a GI sleeping bag outfit consisting of inner and outer eiderdown bags and a waterproof cover.

*Tales of a New England Boyhood*

Through the ensuing years, those bags kept me warm on many a camping or field trip; although not used in recent years, they are still serviceable! The Eagle ceremonies were conducted during my senior year in high school, which was my last year as an active scout and first year of dating the beautiful girl who later consented to be my wife.

This brings to a close a brief narrative about scouting days. Happily, I have kept nearly all documents associated with progress from Tenderfoot through Eagle ranks.

Chief of Police Michael Stewart, president of Scituate Kiwanis Club, presents U.S. Army sleeping bags to new Eagle Scouts at recognition banquet, spring, 1946. Left to right: Cobby Swift, Tom Macy, Chief Stewart, "P" Miles, Donald Hattin.

# Chapter 14
## North Scituate A&P Store

Shortly after reaching my fourteenth birthday I landed my first long-term job, as stockboy and clerk of our local A&P store. This establishment was located in North Scituate Village, across Gannett Road from the NY, NH&H railroad station and next door to the Gates clothing store. During the winter and spring of 1943, my wages amounted to 40¢/hour and I worked after school and on Saturdays, but in the summer of that year my employment was full time. Full time meant nine hours per day for five days each week, and my first real salary – $18 per week. Within a month, that amount was increased to $20, and during the next two summers was raised again to $22 and $24 per week, respectively. These were generous sums for a young man who had just completed the freshman year of high school, had no car, and had no girlfriend. I opened a bank account and was, except for a brief period in 1949, never again without ready cash!

Among my first A&P tasks was the counting and bagging of soiled aprons and smocks, which had to be sent out each week

U.S. Post Office, Gates Dry Goods store, and A&P store (far left), North Scituate Village, ca. 1935. Photo courtesy of Lawrence "Chick" Gates, president of S.H.S. class of 1937, via Paul Miles.

for cleaning. Even this seemed formidable because I kept count in my head rather than keeping score with pencil and paper. Another early assignment was bagging potatoes for our steady customers. When I began work, the U.S. was fully engaged in WWII, and potatoes, though not rationed, were in short supply. Our store (No. 1032 of the A&P chain) received a single 150# barrel of spuds each week, and we had to spread the contents pretty broadly among our regulars. So I made up brown paper bags with either three-pound or two-pound amounts, and these were kept in our stockroom at the rear of the store. When a customer asked for potatoes, Joe, head of our produce department, would call, "Donald," and I would look out toward the front of the store. Just as a baseball catcher might do, Joe would discretely hold down two or three fingers to let me know whether to bring out a two-pound or three-pound bag of these prized items. Among other things, Joe told me to mix fresh green beans with older ones so that the customers had at least a 50/50 chance of picking up a fresh bean when breaking one to test freshness. In those days, we "plugged" watermelons to show customers whether or not the melon was ripe. "Plugging" consisted of making a triangular cut near mid-length of the melon, and then pulling out the resulting wedge so that redness and thickness of rind could be checked. I don't remember anyone ever saying that the melon was not sufficiently ripe, and I don't know what we would have done with a "plugged" melon that had been rejected.

My first year at the store was almost all connected with the produce department, but once a week a semi-trailer load of groceries arrived. A ladder-like device filled with many rollers was laid out from trailer door to stockroom, and all cases or other containers marked 1032 came rolling down into the store. My job was to catch and stack these, usually bucket-brigade fashion with at least one other employee. Commonly, this was the manager, Jim Ward. When all boxes had been unloaded, I commenced delivering them to appropriate places adjacent to the display shelves, which were along the walls behind counters where grocery clerks "waited on trade." The boxes were then opened and the contents stacked neatly in appropriate open spaces on the shelves. Prices were shown in large numerals that were fitted into small metal clips attached to the shelves. Bar codes were far in the future at this time, as were electronic scanners.

The meat and fresh vegetables arrived by express delivery truck. Because of the war, meat was not only rationed but also in very short supply. Typically, our store was allotted one dressed hog and one thigh of beef each week, as well as a plentiful supply of fish, and amounts of salt pork, bacon, and poultry that were adequate for local demand. The red meat was kept in a walk-in refrigerator, and was parceled out to our most loyal customers. Non-regulars and unknowns were simply told that we had no pork or beef. Vegetables and fruit arrived in a variety of containers – barrels for potatoes; flimsy wire-and wood crates for lettuce; sturdy half-bushel boxes for cherries, limes, pomegranates, tomatoes and pears; bushel baskets for peaches; shallow bushel boxes for beans, peas, cauliflower, and cucumbers; deep bushel boxes for apples; two-compartment crates for oranges, grapefruit and lemons; and well-made recyclable, completely enclosed wooden chests for bananas. Invariably, citrus fruit suffered considerable spoilage, and one of my most cherished memories concerns the fate of that fruit. I took all such items, cut out the soft or moldy parts, and squeezed the juice into a one-gallon crock. The mixture, usually containing orange, grapefruit and lemon juice, and sometimes also containing lime juice, was sweetened with about half a cup of sugar – even during the war when sugar was rationed! I placed the crock in the walk-in refrigerator, and as soon as the mixture was well chilled, served it to any of the help who wanted a refreshing drink. Most did! Deeelicious! Pears ripened fast and had to be sold quickly. But in Mr. Wolf, we had an ace in the hole. Because he had no teeth, the dead-ripe pears were just the thing to satisfy his "sweet tooth." Invariably, he asked to sample a pear, and after "gumming" one to death, he bought a half dozen or so to take home. "Sampling" the fruit was accepted practice, and we never charged for the first piece that customers ate. Normally, the "sampling" included cherries, pears and peaches, but never citrus fruit, bananas, or apples. Pomegranates simply did not command much of the market, so I ended up eating about half of all that were delivered to the store. Bing cherries also disappeared at an accelerated rate whenever I was on duty. And peas! The war had little effect on supplies of many kinds of fruit and vegetables, but oranges were a problem, and there were times when we had none. Oranges came in crates labeled "120" if, for example, the crate contained 120 oranges. The low point in our orange supply came when we got crates labeled as high as "280." These were the tiniest oranges I've seen, then or since. Obviously, they weren't good enough for the troops, so civilians received them.

After a year or so in the produce department, I was transferred to the grocery side of the store, and came under the direct supervision of Jim Ward, who was a most benevolent boss. An example of his kindness manifested itself soon after I became salaried. Somewhere up the chain of command came an order for me to join the food-producers' union. Mr. Ward simply opened the till, took out a twenty dollar bill and put it in an envelope, which was then sent to the union. That's the last I ever head from or about the union.

Work in the grocery department was great fun, and put me in a much more responsible position. Prices were marked, but within a month I could recite from memory the prices of hundreds of items, from stove blacking to a box of what was then known as "dry" cereal. Most of the merchandise was behind the counter, so the customer would recite, one at a time, names of items that were desired. As each item was named, that item was taken from its shelf, and the price listed in pencil on a 5#-size paper bag. The pencil, of course, was carried on one's ear when not in use. When all the items had been assembled, the clerk totaled prices with simple addition and the customer handed over that amount. The amount (no checks; credit cards were unheard of) was rung up on a mechanical cash register, the cash drawer popped out, and the money placed in appropriate compartments of the drawer. Groceries were placed in brown paper bags, including the one that had the list of prices. That way the customer could check our addition. All the clerks became truly expert at rapid and correct addition.

One aspect of grocery sales seems quaint by today's rigid sanitary standards. Cookies were delivered loose in cardboard cartons which were about 12" square. Once the carton had been opened, it was fitted with a metal-framed glass door and placed among several others on a set of display shelves. Cookies were sold by weight, and were selected and bagged with our bare hands! Speaking of sanitation, both in the store and at home hamburger was frequently ingested raw, and I don't remember ever getting sick from the practice. Of course, we had to keep the flies in check and did so with dangling strips of flypaper.

During World War II, a great many items were rationed, and families or individuals received ration books containing coupons of various colors for such items as sugar, meat, butter, and certain canned goods. Gasoline was tightly controlled, automobile owners qualifying for A, B, or C ration cards depending upon degree of necessity. Special items, such as tires and bicycles, were also rationed; I recollect that one had to approach the local ration board to get a permit or coupon to buy these. Shoes were also rationed. In the A&P store we were always short of the rationed items, and wouldn't sell any to persons who weren't regular customers. It didn't take long to learn who was who in a town as small as Scituate, the population being only a little over 4,000 persons in 1940. The sugar ration was 5 pounds, but we often had so little that it had to be parceled out in one-pound lots. The butter ration was probably something like a pound per family per week, but we usually dispensed it 1/4 pound per customer. At times, butter arrived not in one-pound cartons but in round tubs, so we had to cut it into 1/4-pound wedges. We always had margarine, but few people cared for it because it came uncolored, presumably so it could not be sold as butter. The margarine was packaged in a plastic bag that contained a packet of orange-colored powder. By breaking the packet of powder and kneading the whole package, the margarine was converted to a yellow color. The stuff didn't taste nearly so much like butter as today's margarine, but folks used plenty of it.

We nearly always had yellow cheese in stock, and I ate lots of it. My favorite kind – called "rat" cheese, but was probably cheddar – came in a large round wooden box, and the whole cheese probably weighed about 10 or 12 pounds. We cut this flavorful cheese into wedges by means of a butcher knife. When

Above: WWII ration stamps entitled bearer to an allotted quantity of scarce food items. Below: War Ration Board instructions regarding dates for using fuel oil and gasoline coupons, stamp valid for one pair of shoes, stamps for foodstuffs, and inspection of tires for those having B and C gasoline ration books.

cheese became really scarce, some less interesting varieties arrived at the store, including one that was covered with black wax and was so hard that we had to hack it into wedges with a meat cleaver. Because of the resulting splintered edges this cheese caused small cuts in the roof of one's mouth, and those cuts stung pretty severely. When cigarettes became scarce, we began to receive cartons of brands we'd never heard of. Instead of Luckies, Camels or Chesterfields, we'd get Rameses, Picayunes, and Wings, the last being o.k., I guess, because my maternal grandmother smoked them. Cigarettes may have been scarce, but the price of "weeds" (as we called them) and nearly everything else remained static because of price controls determined by the O.P.A. (Office of Price Administration). Cigarettes remained at 16¢ a pack or two packs for 31¢ for as long as I worked at the store. Doling out the scarce items was sort of fun because we always seemed to have enough of everything to enable our regular customers to get *some* sugar, *some* potatoes, *some* cigarettes, *some* cheese, *some* red meat, etc., and NO ONE EVER COMPLAINED!

The final routine of the working day was erection of the "tent," which enclosed a small area just inside the front door. This allowed for milk to be delivered early in the morning without permitting access to the entire store. The "tent" comprised a three-sided affair that was held up by steel pipes inserted into floor holes so as to form supports for the resulting wall of stout brown canvas. For me, the first chores of the morning were to roll up the tent against one side of the door and place the milk inside the cooler. Of course, in those days milk and cream always came in glass bottles. Another of my tasks was to tend the furnace during the colder months. Water level was controlled by a valve and monitored by means of a sight glass, just as in a steam locomotive. The fire was banked at night, which meant closing the dampers and adding a few scoops of coal to the now slow-burning fire. In the morning, the grates had to be shaken gently so as not to drop the little bit of remaining fire, and fresh coal had to be added. The dampers were opened to increase the draft, and water had to be added to the boiler. Slowly, the heated water rose into the store's three radiators (yes, just three), which did no more than take off the chill. During most winter days, it was necessary to wear warm shirts or sweaters under our white smocks. One of the biggest problems in tending the fire was getting to the furnace without getting wet. The basement of No. 1032 was almost always awash with from 1 to 3 inches of water, even more after a heavy rain. A series of heavy wooden gingerale boxes served in the fashion of stepping stones to reach the furnace. That basement was a really dreary place in any season, and the thought of having to go down there is one of my least cherished memories of the A&P store.

Many happier things occurred at the store, among the most memorable of which was the occasional arrival of a truly beautiful young woman who was rumored to be a welder in one of the two nearby shipyards. One hot summer day she actually arrived barefoot, wearing only an undersized two-piece bathing suit that furnished more than mere glimpses of her voluptuous body. I doubt that such a display, commonplace after the Bikini bomb blast, had ever been seen previously in North Scituate, and was certainly demonstrative beyond the mores of that time. As she walked through the store, every head of the help and customers alike turned, and all conversation dropped to zero. If she was looking for attention, it was given in abundance. The swim suit was of a pale purple color, but it sure wasn't the color that was attracting so much interest!

Another of my duties was carrying filled grocery sacks to customer's cars, or on occasion, even to their homes. Regarding this, I remember one summer resident, an older single lady, who invariably said, "Donald, my car is right outside, number 12109." She was related in some way to Mr. Gilday, who was a higher level supervisor for several A&P stores on the South Shore. She always tried to tip me, but I routinely refused because such assistance was a simple courtesy to our customers. However, on one occasion, after I had loaded a huge carton of toilet paper into the automobile of Mr. Brazilian, who ran the Cliff Hotel in Minot, that gentleman slipped some coins into my shirt pocket and turned away before I could protest. That was the only tip I have ever received!

During those intervals when trade was slow, the clerks, a majority of whom were of high-school age, walked next door to Brook's Pharmacy, which was managed by the very pleasant and accomodating pharmacist, Ruth Bartlett. There, we ordered fountain concoctions – milk shakes, frappes, etc. – and sat in one of the booths reading comic books until the break, usually only ten minutes, was over. Ruth let each of us run a weekly tab, which we dutifully paid on Saturday after receiving our week's wages (in cash).

A final flurry of daily activity occurred at about the time the steam-powered train arrived from Boston with its load of commuters (see photo in Chapter 11). We closed promptly at 6:00 p.m., swept the floors, turned out the lights, erected the "tent" inside the front door, and went our separate ways. For me, the journey home was usually on my red, balloon-tired, one-speed bicycle – a trip I made for the last time in the fall of 1945.

Late in the spring of 1946 I interviewed a local truck gardener, Bernard Meyers, for a job on his farm. Happily, I got the job, and for the next three growing seasons experienced one of the most satisfying jobs of my youth (see Chapter 18).

# Chapter 15
## Lobster Fishing

Mr. Jim Ward, for whom I worked at the North Scituate A&P store, inherited from his father a well-crafted wooden lobstering boat that was one of the so-called "white fleet" based at Scituate harbor. With World War II going well for the allies, Mr. Ward could envision lobstering as a profitable sideline as early as spring, 1945. Preparations included refurbishment of the boat, "building" lobster pots (= traps), painting approximately 200 wooden buoys that would mark trap locations, and cutting lengths of rope that would join pot and buoy in the 60 or so feet of water that were to be "fished." During the winter and spring of 1944/1945 Jim hired me to do after-school and weekend work on the pots and buoys, while he and his wife, Doris, knitted heads (= nets) that would form entrances to the two compartments within each pot. The buoys were cut to 24" lengths from 4x4 wood stock. One end was beveled and drilled for attaching "pot warp," a type of water-resistant rope about ⅜" in diameter. Working in the Ward's basement, I mixed white paint that was a concoction of white lead, turpentine, and linseed oil. Each new buoy was given three coats of this paint. Next, I painted identifying color bands on the end opposite the rope hole. The color scheme was blue, red, blue, with one inch of white paint showing between the color bands, each of which was painted all the way around the buoy. The lobster pots had a flat bottom and rounded top, the basic frame being available commercially. The ends were open, and slats along the sides extended only half the length of the unfinished pot, leaving two side openings. My job was to affix a large head across the inside of the new pot, midway between the two ends, so as to create an inner chamber. Next, smaller heads were attached to each of the side openings that were positioned in the other half of the pot. Mr. and Mrs. Ward had woven a metal hoop, about 5 inches in diameter, into the center of each "head." Later, these heads would be stretched tautly by heavy twine fastened to these steel hoops. After nailing the heads in place, I wired two bricks into the bottom of each pot. These would counteract buoyancy when the pot was dropped into the sea. Finally, a heavy copper-wire hook was fastened to the inside of the inner chamber. Fish heads fastened to these hooks would serve as bait to attract lobsters. Once the heads, bricks and bait hook were in place, I nailed slats across each end of the pot, thus completing the trap. Lastly, the head leading to the inner chamber was drawn tightly towards the end of the pot by means of stout twine, and the two smaller heads were drawn tautly towards each other by twine attached to each of their steel rings. Thus tightened, each of the three heads formed a funnel-like opening, two of these leading to the entrance chamber, the third leading to the inner chamber. Now the pot was ready for use.

Jim had the pots delivered to the town pier at Scituate Harbor, transferred them to his boat, and set them out in a series of trap lines a mile or so offshore. Each line of pots had to be tended every couple of days. For this work I served willingly as deckhand. At 5:30 a.m. on trap-tending days, Jim and his wife picked me up at my home and the three of us proceeded to the town pier. Jim then rowed out to get his lobster boat and brought it to the pier. Using smelly fish heads, which were brought down in barrels from Boston, I pitchforked the heads from the pier down into a wooden barrel that sat on the boat deck. This worked fine at high tide, but at low tide, the boat was far below pier level and many heads missed the barrel and splattered stinky goo across the deck. However, the boat engine powered a hose which we used to wash away this slop. Finally, we began our trip out of the harbor – rain or shine, windy or calm, foggy or clear! As we passed the bellbuoy which marks the harbor entrance, Jim lined up Lawson Tower and the

Goulston Company smokestack, set the throttle at a particular position, and timed our run. After a certain number of minutes, we knew that one or another of the pot lines was at hand, and sure enough, we'd soon spot one of the red, white, and blue-banded buoys. As Jim maneuvered the boat close, I reached overside with a gaff and hooked the rope and buoy. Pulling this aboard, I handed the buoy and rope to Jim, who flipped the rope onto a davit-mounted pulley, then placed a couple turns of rope around the engine-driven winch. By exerting a little tension on the free end, the winch took hold of the rope and began to raise the pot. When the pot reached the surface I hauled it aboard, opened the lid and removed the lobsters, crushed any crabs (sometimes there were many), placed a "new" fish head on the bait hook, then closed and latched the lid. As soon as Jim had pegged the lobsters' claws and dropped them into the "live well" of circulating sea water, he engaged the gears and gave the Gray marine engine some throttle. As the boat gained speed, I pushed the pot overboard, the rope singing over the starboard gunwhale as we pulled away. It was *essential* not to step on the loosely coiled rope as it lay on deck in order that it would pay out without becoming tangled. Repeating this process until we reached the end of the trap line, Jim then steered the boat homeward, frequently with two or more bushels of fine fresh decapods on board.

On some days, heavy fog blanketed the sea, but we had little trouble finding the pot line even when landmarks were invisible. On such days, the water surface had a smooth, glassy appearance and the swells were usually small. During one bright sunny day, a brisk southwest wind gradually increased, causing swells 6 to 7 feet high, or more. When we reached the northern end of the trap line and headed for the harbor we faced directly into these waves, which were very close together. The boat rose up steeply over one wave and literally dove under the next, such that a sheet of green water came washing over the foredeck. This water hit us hard, and I remember hanging on tightly to a handrail that ran across the aft end of the foredeck. This was an exhilarating experience, and I loved very minute of it. Each day, when our boat returned to the town pier, we unloaded the catch, which was then hand delivered directly to various homes at 40¢ per pound. The largest lobster we caught that summer was a 7 pounder – too large for me to pick up with one hand. One of the greatest perquisites of my lobster-fishing summer was taking home any lobsters which lacked one of the large claws or was of legal length but too small to be salable. My family ate *lots* of lobsters that summer! We were usually off the water by 11:00 a.m., and each day I received wages of $5.00, about double the amount of most hourly jobs at that time!

While we were on the water, Doris furnished crackers and gingerale, the latter served in small glass tumblers. She was particular about keeping track of whose glass was whose. A good thing too, because Jim coughed a great deal. At the time, I thought it was because of his smoking, but he was later diagnosed as having tuberculosis. Eventually, in 1947 or 1948, I was told that he had been cured of T.B. but had succumbed to cancer. Having spent a lot of time with Jim in the A&P store, in his home, and on the water, I felt a sincere sense of loss at his passing. He was a kind, gentle and generous man.

# Chapter 16
## First Baptist Church And A Close Call

Only twice in my boyhood did I see Dad in a church. The first instance was during a sightseeing visit to the Old Indian church in Mashpee, MA, the second being in Scituate's St. Mary's, to which the family had been invited by a Catholic relative. My mom did a little better; she was an Easter person, suggesting something less than full devotion to organized religion. Despite these seeming deficiencies, Sunday School attendance was mandatory for the Hattin children. So, rain or shine, dressed in go-to-meeting clothes and usually with no small measure of prodding (at least for me), we walked a quarter mile to North Scituate's First Baptist Church to attend services. (See photo in Chapter 11) Why that church? Well, neither of my parents had been brought up as Baptists, but proximity to our home made the choice pretty obvious.[1]

---

[1] For reasons I shall never know I was promoted from the Cradle Roll Department to the Beginners Department of the First Congregational church of Wrentham, MA, in 1933! This was *two years* after our family had moved from Egypt, MA, to North Scituate. Strange!

My earliest Sunday School classes were held in the so-called "middle vestry," where the always-present collection device was a small ceramic teacup – red on the inner surface and gilded on the outer. Dr. and Mrs. Max D. Miles had brought this home from Burma, where they had been in missionary service for several years. That cup; into which we dropped our pennies, nickels, or dime [sic]; is one of two lasting memories from my earliest brush with theistic principles and practices. The other is the Lord's prayer, which in my childhood version ended with the words, "for Thine is the kingdom, and the *parlor*, and the glory, forever. Amen."

A totally different aspect of church activity manifested itself during summertime Bible School, which attracted Protestant and Catholic kids alike. Mainly, we seemed to make things, the most memorable being a doorstop featuring a cat's face cut from plywood with a coping saw, painted (bright yellow, in my work), then affixed in upright position to a wooden wedge. Pretty neat! Mary Bailey supervised my groups, but there were many adult helpers as well as older neighborhood boys, the latter including Mooney Dorr and Richard Fleming. One memorable activity involved an attempt to learn outdoor cooking. Somehow, Mary transported my class to the water-filled excavation off Route 3-A that was known to all as "the pit."

Donald E. Hattin

First Baptist Church Bible School class, ca. 1936.

L to r: at far left of back row: Mary Bailey, Mooney Dorr, Doc Creelman.

Supplied with a kettle, milk, onion, salt, and a potato, each team of two was given instructions on how to kindle a fire, prepare the ingredients, and end up with delicious, hot potato soup. My teammate was David Schultz. We decided to build our fire in a quiet nook between two large boulders, and soon had a nice blaze underway. Next, we placed milk, salt, cut-up potato and onion into the kettle and propped it up with small stones. At this point we were suddenly surrounded by a swarm of very angry bees which had no inclination to let us continue. In our cleverness to find a sheltered spot for the fire we had unwittingly smoked these insects from their hideout, and were forced to beat a hasty retreat. When I grew a little older, Mary asked me to help a group of ten- or eleven-year-olds with bookcase construction. As a bonus, I also got to build one, and put it to good use throughout the remainder of my days in Scituate. When we sold our home, the bookcase went with it.

As early teenagers, my crowd had Sunday School classes in the main vestry, where the affable and talented Evan Bailey commanded what he called "Daniel's Band." Each of us had to memorize, in order, names of all books in the Bible. What earthly purpose was served thereby remains for me a great mystery, but I can still remember the order of the first seven books, and by age seventy seven had finally read the first four and had got partway through Deuteronomy. On the first Christmas with Evan, each member of the our class received a pencil on which was impressed and gilded the words "Daniel's Band." On the second Christmas, Evan gave each of us; including Sarge Bartlett, Paul Miles, Charles Fleming, Cobby and Punch Swift, etc.; a large and powerful rat trap. Brown rats did exist in the neighborhood, but not in such numbers as to require widespread persecution. Apparently, Evan believed we ought have rat traps, and we thanked him for such thoughtfulness. Within 5 minutes of opening these perilous gifts, Punch succeeded in springing his trap onto his thumb, thereby seriously mangling the nail and causing so much pain that he had great difficulty suppressing a copious flow of tears. All I want to know is this: how did Evan know we needed rat traps?

Next in the order of Baptist Church involvement came affiliation with a youth group known as Christian Endeavor. How I got roped into this activity is recounted in the chapter entitled "Scouting Adventures." Once there, my heart was lost to Margie Macy, the engaging fourteen-year-old girl about whom we first learned in Chapter 7. Losing initial trepidation, I soon found myself looking forward eagerly to the weekly C.E. meetings, in no small measure owing to Margie's regular attendance. As time passed, I actually lead one or two of the meetings, using a lesson plan furnished by our adult leader Merrill Merritt, or later, Bob Cowdrey. In addition to meetings, which were held in the "back" or "rear" vestry, we had occasional outside activities, most memorable among which was a picnic served on a long table set up in the side yard of the Swift home. There were perhaps twelve of us in attendance, and the main dish was spaghetti and meatballs. As we turned towards dessert, I remarked on the quantity of food that remained on some plates. Intending it as a joke, one of our gang suggested that perhaps I should eat the leftover food rather than having it go to waste. This was more of a dare than concern that my spare frame required additional sustenance. Without hesitation, I accepted the challenge and cleaned off the offending plates, thereby demonstrating my belief that all of these friends were living up to the strictest of hygienic standards!

Because of involvement with Christian Endeavor, I began regular attendance at Sunday morning services, and actually enjoyed the Reverend Creelman's often overlong sermons without falling asleep. Once each month, we had a communion service, with the traditional bread and grape juice ritual. Why grape juice, I wondered? At the last supper, Jesus and his disciples drank wine, so why shouldn't we do the same? Apropos of this discrepancy, I recall that during each communion Sunday the attendees read, in unison, a tract known as "the covenant." One phrase exhorted us to abstain from the use of alcoholic beverages. Wishing to avoid hypocrisy, a large majority of the congregation did not speak this phrase, and the decibel level dropped by at least 85 percent!

As the 1945-46 school year progressed I felt increasingly drawn into the religious orbit, even to the point of full-immersion baptism, and decided to talk seriously to "Doc" Creelman about a career in the ecclesiastical realm. At the parsonage, Doc and I had a meeting about which my friends were so excited that they gave me the new and not entirely unwarranted nickname, "Deacon Don." What Doc told me about seminary, ordination, placement, duties, salary, etc., sapped forever any enthusiasm for a life in the cloth. With my ministerial ambitions shattered, the euphonious nickname quickly faded from memory.

# Chapter 17
## Sentimental Journey

From the day I first laid eyes on Margie Macy, she became the foremost thing in my thoughts. Never mind that prior to this event boy scouting had occupied nearly all my spare time, and I had had absolutely no interest in girls. But a North Scituate lad had already taken her to the movies a couple of times, and was paired with her for a mid-winter Christian Endeavor hayride, which for me was a completely miserable experience. Finally, while babysitting for a family living just a few doors from my home, I mustered sufficient courage to call Margie just to say, "hello," and to talk. What she thought of this I cannot guess, but at least she wasn't offended. At this time I was freckle-faced, blinked a lot, and hardly ever combed my hair – a decidedly irresistible combination!

Eventually, her boyfriend of the 1944/1945 winter dropped from the scene, and by springtime she had accepted an invitation from "P" Miles to attend the junior prom, which was held at Tom Lawson's former home, Dreamwold Hall. Of course, I went stag, and bided my time while drinking "tonic," eating cake, and listening to a pretty fair "big band." Newest in their repertoire was "Sentimental Journey," and I longed to dance to this tune with the girl of my dreams. At last, with all the courage I could gather, I cut in on "P" and Margie, and danced for about half a minute before the bandleader announced an intermission. To my everlasting gratitude "P" did not reclaim his date, instead allowing me to sit with her for the entire break. She was dressed in a beautiful blue evening gown sewn by Mrs. Macy, and wore a pearl and sapphire necklace. This wonderful girl was actually sitting with me and talking with me. I was

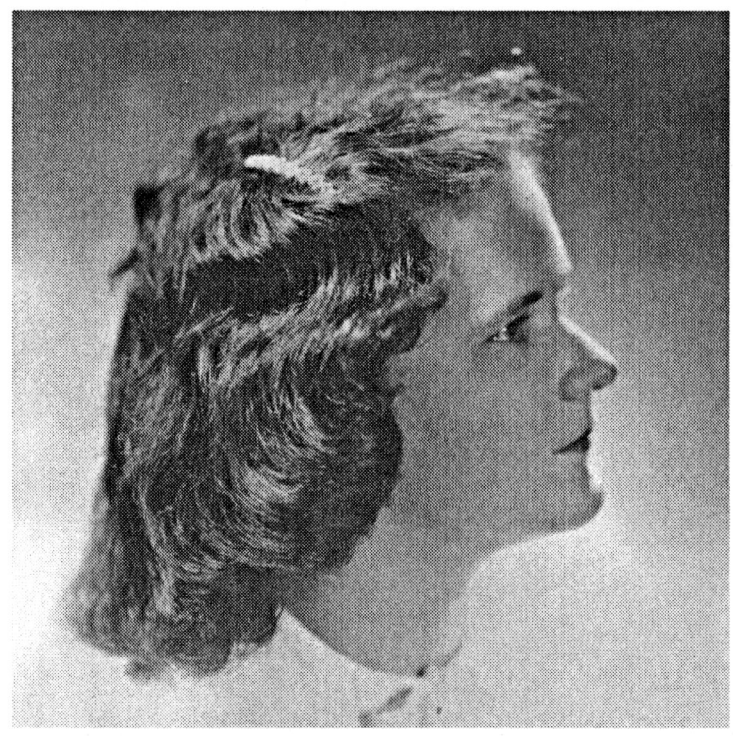

Margie Macy, 1948.

floating on a cloud! By the end of intermission, I had asked her to be my date for the upcoming senior reception. She said that she would, and I could hardly believe that after all these months my dream of dating her would finally come true.

Before the big dance, another dance took place, at the high school. Of course, I asked Margie to be my date for that event. There was, however, a rather serious problem – I did not own a pair of dress shoes. Mrs. Harry Chipman, a great friend of my mom's, learned of this dilemma and volunteered use of a pair of Harry's shoes. I accepted, but discovered that the shoes were a half size too small and a size or so too narrow. Nonetheless, I polished them carefully, and together with "Punch" Swift and his date, Jeannie, drove to the dance in the Swift's "jeep." While dancing with Margie my feet were killing me, so I went downstairs to the boys' locker room, took off the offending footgear, and donned my athletic sneakers. Although these were more comfortable, pivoting maneuvers were less than smooth, but not a soul noticed the change. Back at the Macy's doorstep after the dance, I asked Margie if we could kiss – this on our *first* date. She agreed. Hoping beforehand that this might happen, I had wondered to myself, "When kissing, where do the noses go?" Well, our first-ever kiss answered *that* question!

About the senior prom, I recall only that Margie wore a lovely yellow gown, also sewn by her talented mother, and wore the gardenia corsage I had bought. Again, the band played "Sentimental Journey," which from that night onward has been "our song." After the dance, we went to a favorite Hingham hangout named "Page's," and at evening's end we kissed again at the Macy doorstep. By this time, I was definitely an old hand at this sort of thing.

Throughout my senior year (Margie was a sophomore) we dated frequently, usually with at least one other couple, and driving either in Swift's "jeep" or in a sedan owned by the Varney family. Fortunately, the end of WWII brought a halt to gasoline rationing, but our travels rarely extended farther than Nantasket, where rides in Paragon Park were perennial favorites, especially the bumper cars.

In school, Margie and I often passed notes while filing from one class to another. Ridiculous as it now seems, such behavior was forbidden, but we delighted in doing so and were never "caught." After school, Margie and I walked to her home, usually by way of Lawson Road and Captain Pierce Road. On one occasion, as we passed Egypt Post Office, Donald Bickford rode by on his bicycle and hollered, "Puppy love!" He could hardly envision that we would still be together more than sixty years later.

Margie's love for gardenias prompted my occasional after school visits to Fred Waterman's greenhouse on First Parish Road. He always had fresh gardenias in the cooler, and after purchasing one I'd walk nearly two miles to the Macy home and present this gift to my sweetheart. Once, this took place on a snowy day when the streets were full of slush, and I had nothing on my feet except a pair of ordinary low-quarter shoes. Needless to say, by the time I reached home, after walking more than three miles, my shoes were soggy, my feet were cold, and I was soaked – and happy!

Margie and the author on a fall walk, 1946.

Margie and I took many long walks together. In fine weather, we always walked to her home following Sunday afternoon meetings of Christian Endeavor, and took many a walk along the shore, where she sometimes rode on my shoulders. Another hike involved visiting a huge beech tree in the woods off the upper end of Booth Hill Road. There, we dutifully carved our initials on the beech, which was universally known as "the initial tree." Across the street from my home was a long driveway leading up to the home of Mr. and Mrs. Job Vinal. Near their house grew a dandy climbing tree – a sugar maple – from upper branches of which the ocean could be glimpsed. Naturally, Margie needed to see this tree, and we did climb it one day in the fall of 1945.

On another fall day in 1945, Margie and I walked to her home from school, and decided to go for a bike ride. We had to go to my home to pick up a second bike, so she rode while I walked. Margie's bike was a wartime model, purchased by application to the town ration board, which approved on basis of her need to have transportation to work (she had a job at the Goulston Company plant on Hatherly Road). As she pedaled along the upper end of Ann Vinal Road, with me jogging alongside, I reached out to hold onto one of the handlebars. This caused an imbalance, and to my great consternation Margie crashed to the ground and suffered a severely abraded, bleeding right forearm. Knowing that return to her home just three hundred yards behind us would end our outing, she stoically decided to continue. At my home, Margie had her first opportunity to meet my mother, who cleaned and dressed the wound before we took the planned bike ride. This was one of the few times that my mom ever saw the girl who would one day be my wife.

Christmas, 1945, would be the first time Margie and I exchanged presents, and I hadn't a clue as to what she might like. Cobby Swift told me he'd purchased for Jan Allen, his future wife, a nice present at Danny Campbell's boutique in the neigh-

Margie Macy visiting the author's home, winter, 1945/1946.

boring town of Cohasset. Seizing upon this idea, I biked to Cohasset Village and at the store asked Danny for suggestions. He showed me a beautiful pair of slipper socks – leather soles and colorful knit uppers – which I believed were just perfect. On Christmas day, Margie told me that Cobby had bought Jan the identical gift!

Swift's "jeep" was a unique vehicle for dating (see photo in Chapter 13). With three rows of seats and a chain-supported tailgate, it was not uncommon for us to "quadruple" date because few of our gang had ready (or any) access to a car. During winter months, dating in the open-sided "jeep" required warm clothing and sometimes a blanket. Margie's mother invariably asked, "Won't you be cold?" to which Margie invariably replied

Girlfriends: Janet Allen (left) and Margie Macy, on the Macy front lawn, 1945.

with an unconvincing, "No." Thanks to the Swift brothers, with whom we usually double or triple dated, the open-sided jeep became one of Margie's and my most enduring and treasured memories. We continued dating for five years, were married on July 15, 1950, and commenced a life filled with travel, adventure, and a generous measure of family happiness.

# Chapter 18
## Ben Meyers' Farm

After three years at the A&P store, the time had come to seek new employment challenges; therefore, on a tip from classmate Jack Litchfield, I went to ask truck gardener Bernard Meyers if he had need for another field hand. The interview took place in the den of The Beeches, his lovely home on Curtis Street. This was one of the many gambrel-roofed, cedar-shingled houses built in Egypt, MA, by well-remembered multi-millionaire Thomas W. Lawson. Ben, who was resting on a couch, heard my request and said he'd let me know. Later, I learned that he never hired anyone without first mentioning an applicant's name to the boys already in his employ, and watching and listening closely as they made their comments. Any hesitation spelled rejection. The boys' reaction to my application must have been favorable. Just two or three days after the interview, I received a message from Ben's son, Elden, that his dad wanted me to start work on the following Saturday. This was during the spring of 1946, and school was still in session, so Saturdays, plus a

*Tales of a New England Boyhood*

"The Beeches," home of Ben Meyers and his family on Curtis Street, Egypt, MA, ca. 1938. Photo courtesy of Ben's granddaughter, Laurianne Olcott.

couple hours after school each day, constituted the remunerative work week at about 75¢ per hour.

Ben's farm comprised a collection of fields, which were known by names of the owners or by an important landmark. Acreage is hard to recollect, but none of these fields exceeded about four or five acres, and two were less than an acre. Two fields were situated on Captain Pierce Road, adjacent to the Edward White home, and one of the largest fields lay adjacent to Lawson Tower. The Chase field lay off Orchard Road, the Egypt field lay beside the New Haven railroad tracks northeast of the Egypt railroad station, the Rencurrel field lay at the end of Hillside Road, the small Watts field lay behind Watts' barn off Captain Pierce Road, and a final sizeable field lay behind the Gardner home, off Tilden Road. The smallest field lay behind the Sibley home, off Hillside Road, and was approached by way of the Rencurrel field. We called it the Sibley Field, which was totally surrounded by woods. Thus, our work was spread over nine separate fields, each of which we came to know with great intimacy. The names and locations of these fields are mentioned here because their names appear below in connection with various incidents of farm life, which was as happy a series of events as a teenage boy could possibly experience.

During one of my first afternoons on the farm, we were all hoeing cauliflowers in the Chase field when the subject of trade unions somehow came into our collective conversation. I ventured the opinion that the iron grip of unionism was having

The White field, off Captain Pierce road near Egypt railroad station, planted in cucumbers, ca. 1940. Tower, upper left, furnished water to the White family home. Photo courtesy of Laurianne Olcott.

a very bad effect on prices of goods, the speed of construction, etc., and that unionism was even undermining the work ethic what with constant demands for shorter work weeks, strike pay, and exclusion of non-union workers from certain parts of the job force. Well! I sure had touched the wrong nerve, because Ben really began to tear my argument to shreds. Ben had been brought up in the coal fields of western Pennsylvania, and had been employed in many aspects of mining as well as in the Pittsburgh steel mills. In each instance, he had worked his way up to supervisory rank in the trade unions, which he regarded as absolutely essential to the well being of union members. He told of miners having to buy their own tools and dynamite, and of being forced to buy everything in company stores. It was a story that later was symbolized in the Tennessee Ernie Ford song that ended, "I owe my soul to the company store." My thoughts were hypothetical, but Ben's were empirical. From that day to this, my views on trade unions have never been the same!

The precision with which Ben farmed his fields should have become a Scituate legend. Initially, let us look at cauliflowers. First, a field that Ben had plowed and harrowed was then marked with what looked like a giant wooden rake. In order to do this, Ben strung a taut line along one edge of the field, then dragged this huge rake along the line so that the teeth, set 3 feet apart, scored a series of grooves in the soft earth. Using the groove farthest from the taut line as a guide, he then dragged the rake the other way, with one tooth following the pre-existing groove and the other teeth making several additional grooves. When the entire field had thus been scored, planting began. Several teams were engaged in this process, each team consisting of four people, all schoolboys except Ben (behind his back we called him "Benny").[1] These four proceeded in succession down one of the grooves. Using a thick, sharpened club, the first guy punched holes at about 2-foot intervals. The second dropped a small cauliflower plant into the hole. The third poured a can of water into the hole, the water being dipped from a 2 ½ gallon bucket, and the last person set the plant upright, pushed dirt around it, and then tamped the dirt firmly with his fingers. In a few hours, a field of 30,000 cauliflowers was thus planted. Water for the plants came from a wooden tank, which was mounted on a Model A Ford chassis that had the wheels mounted inside out so the wheels could neatly straddle two rows. Once the plants were growing, and nearly every one of them did, we kept the weeds down with hoes that had tiny

---

[1] Ben's son Elden was so much like his dad that we called him "Little Benny."

blades. These were all that remained of standard-sized garden-hoe blades after many years of heavy use. Five or six of us, including Ben and Elden, worked side-by-side, one to a row, hoeing around and between each of the plants. The first year I was on the farm we did all the weeding with hoes, but during my second and third years we used two hand-held cultivators. Such cultivators were designed originally for use with a horse, but by means of a wooden drawbar on a small Farmall tractor, we used two of these cultivators simultaneously. By increasing the spread of these cultivators to nearly three feet, we used them so effectively that by my third year on the farm we no longer needed to hoe the fields.

Once the cauliflower plants began to show a tiny white head, we had to tie up the leaves to prevent the heads from getting

Ben Meyers standing behind wooden tank on stripped-down Model A Ford water truck, ca. 1940. Photo courtesy of Laurianne Olcott.

Ben Meyers (right) and his son, Elden, ca. late 1940's. Model A Ford truck (background) was used for local transport of farmhands and equipment. Photo courtesy of Laurianne Olcott.

"sunburned," or yellowed. On a given day, Ben gave each of us a bundle of 100 strings, each about 24" long, and all of the same color. With one of us per row, we started tying up the leaves of any plant that was beginning to expose the head. Two days later, we repeated the process, only with another color string. Regardless of the weather, these cauliflower leaves had to be tied. I remember occasions when we had to wear slickers and so'westers while tying cauliflowers during high winds and heavy rains! Mostly, however, I remember that the hundreds of tyings cut a deep, painful notch in the thumb side of my right forefinger. About two weeks after the first tying, we entered the field with small, long-handled hatchets and began an every-other-day harvesting routine – cauliflowers with the initial string color being cut first. The cauliflowers were heaped on a truck and taken to Ben's back yard, where he and only the most trusted cutters, usually himself and Jack Litchfield, trimmed off the leaves and packed the snow white heads into wooden bushel boxes – 4,5,9 or 16 heads per box. Great care had to be taken so as not to "scalp" the head by slicing off a part of its naturally lumpy surface. So intense was all of this work that Richie Rencurrel and I composed the following ditty:

> Oh cauliflower, oh cauliflower,
>
> Your leaves are green, your head is white,
>
> At 6:00 a.m., you're a hell of a sight,
>
> Oh cauliflower, oh cauliflower,
>
> When the price is good,
>
> The boss is in a good mood.

Tomatoes, squash and cucumbers were planted in a grid of 5-foot squares. To arrange this pattern, Ben scored the field in one direction with a giant rake having teeth spaced 5 feet apart, then scored the field at right angles to the grooves, also at 5-foot spacing. The planting process was much the same as for cauliflower – punch a hole, drop a plant, pour in water, erect plant and close the hole. As with cauliflower, we did a lot of hoeing that first year (1946), but during my second and third years, the team of Litchfield, Hattin & Rencurrel got so good with the hand-guided cultivators, opened to nearly 5-foot width, that we did almost no hoeing of these plants. Because of the 5x5 grid, we could cross cultivate the plants, sparing almost no weeds and leaving behind a field that presented a beautiful pattern of diagonal rows of plants in several directions! Because of potential problems with insects, the cucumber and squash plants required extensive spraying. Spray was furnished by John Ford, who was also town tree warden. The spray was mixed in a wooden tank mounted on his flatbed truck, and a gasoline-powered pump furnished pressure for delivery. When refilling the pump motor with gasoline, John never bothered to extinguish his cigarette! We hauled literally hundreds of feet of rubber garden-type hose down the rows, and John handled the spray nozzle, spraying a several acre field in a very few hours. During the operation all of us inhaled quite a bit of spray mist.

These plants also required fertilizing and dusting. Fertilizer was applied bare handed by dropping a ring of the granular substance around each of the growing plants. Dusting was carried out with a back-mounted canister of dust operated by a lever and delivery hose *or* by shaking the dust from a porous cloth bag, one shake per plant. I remember well how much of that dust we inhaled into our lungs, especially when the wind was blowing in the same direction we were walking. I can't say that it did any of us much harm because Jack, Richie and I are still around nearly 60 years later!

Harvesting tomatoes was lots of fun. Each of us carried a salt shaker, and when we found an especially nice, ripe tomato would salt and eat it with gusto, sometimes five or six tomatoes each per day. We picked the tomatoes at first blush of orange so that by the time they reached the market place they would be completely red and ripe. If, on a given picking, we missed a few pickable tomatoes, they'd be dead ripe a couple days later when we next entered the field. These weren't marketable, so we either ate them in the field or took them home with us after work. Some of the "dead ripes" were used to remove the blackish-green crust of tomato stain that was all over our hands by day's end. We simply smashed a couple of those beautiful fruits between our hands and washed off the stain with the juice. One other use was effected on a day when I had asked to have an afternoon off so I could take Margie to a play at the Schubert Theater in Boston. We went there and back by train and subway. The next morning, when we met at Benny's to start the day's work, the boys looked a little sheepish. They told me that they had accumulated nearly two bushels of "dead ripes" in the Egypt field, and had carried them to the edge of track owned by the New York, New Haven and Hartford RR. When a train came by, they let fly with over a hundred tomatoes and plastered the passenger cars with tomato puree. Shortly afterward, the town police car, tall antenna waving, drove down into the field, and officer Tony Bongarzone apprehended the miscreants. As Richie reported, Tony got on the radio and said, "Hey Chief, you know the boys that threw the tomatoes at the train? Well, I got em!" Later the boys were brought into the police station accompanied by Jack Litchfield's dad, who worked for the railroad. All were admonished, but no jail sentences were meted out. We had a lot of laughs about it thereafter.

Cucumbers ripened late in the summer, and we usually ate a few of those during harvesting days. When we missed a proper-sized cucumber, by next picking it would have grown too big for marketing. We called these "bulls." One day Jack Litchfield hollered out, "Bulls, boys, bulls," holding up a super-sized specimen which was about 16" long and 4" in diameter! Because of low prices when cucumbers were a glut on the market, Ben had us store scores, maybe hundreds, of bushel boxes in the lower level of Edward White's barn. Every few days we sorted through all of these boxes, removing cucumbers which had spoiled. Such cucumbers were essentially bags of water, and when dropped made a sound like "sploot." The remaining cukes got quite limber, and we called them "Benny's rubber cukes." When the market price rose high enough, the rubber cukes were trucked to market in Boston. Occasionally, we boys would drive a loaded truck to Boston, deliver the contents to a produce wholesaler, and then go to the Old Howard theater on Scollay Square to see a show. The Old Howard had once been a legitimate theatre, but in our youth had become a widely known house of burlesque. The music was tinny, the jokes were corny,

Ford V-8 flatbed market truck loaded with more than 270 bushel boxes of cauliflower, and ready for delivery to Boston, MA, 1946. Left to right: Elden (sitting on cab roof), Ben, the author, Richie Rencurrel. Driver unidentified. Photo courtesy of Laurianne Olcott.

but the girls were a sight to behold – only two pasties and a tiny G-string at the end of a performance!

According to Ben, each of us had a specialty at which he was really good. Jack Litchfield's was trimming cauliflower, Richie's was cultivating, and mine was raking seed beds. The last was accomplished by raking and re-raking a proposed seed bed for cauliflower plants so as to remove all the pebbles that are so typical of Scituate's glacially-influenced soils. A properly raked seed bed comprised smooth, soft, pebble-free loam; I admit to being pretty good at this work.

During the summer, when the weather was hot, we ended the day by showering behind Ben's garage. Each morning he filled an elevated 55-gallon drum with water, and let the sun heat it all day so that we could wash off accumulated dirt at day's end. Occasionally, when the weather was really hot, and we'd put in a good morning's work, Ben would say, "Let's take the afternoon off, and go to the beach." And to the beach we'd go, in one of the big flatbed trucks. Even the boss would sometimes don a swimsuit and join in the watery fun. Those afternoon's off were *with pay*! Ben Meyers was a great guy to work for, always putting in a solid day's work himself, and was generous to a fault. Working for him was the best part-time job I ever had!!

# Chapter 19
## Secondary School

Commencing studies in junior high school was not the traumatic experience which an eleven-year-old boy might have expected. After all, many of my fellow neophytes were friends from Hatherly School days. Right from the beginning, I was assigned to the bus driven by West End farmer Prescott A. Damon, with pickup point being next door to our home at the driveway entrance of that school. From the fall of 1940 through spring of 1946, Damon's was definitely the bus of choice, because Prescott commonly ran late, giving his passengers a valid excuse for tardy arrival. On opening day, 1940, seventh graders were quickly classified alphabetically. Those with last names initialed A-L being assigned to homeroom 7A, Miss Elizabeth Giles in command; and the M-Z's to room 7B, the domain of Miss Dorothy Maxim. Depending on subject matter, we shifted between rooms 7A, 7B, 8A, 8B and a downstairs art room presided over by Miss Doris Rowell.

Seventh grade boys were privileged to take classes in the manual training shop of Mr. Nels Sandberg, a master craftsman who taught the safe, proper, and productive use of various hand tools. Our first project was a wooden water pump, which was to serve as base for a small table lamp, with pump handle serving to pull the light chain on and off. Shop was a two-year requirement, but I opted for three, and altogether completed a candle sconce, nifty footstool, a hinged-top tool chest, and a 2-foot by 3-foot writing table. Several projects required the use of dowels, some the use of dovetailed joints, and all the use of glue. Finished pieces were first stained, then shellacked, smoothed with steel wool and waxed. Thanks to Mr. Sandberg's watchful eye and infinite patience, these products were handsome pieces of which one could be justifiably proud. On the bottom of each completed item, the maker signed his name. Before graduation, one of our neighbors, Mrs. Guy Molinari, purchased my table for $3.00. I still have the tool chest!

In Miss Giles' class (we called her "Lizzie" or "Gilesie") I spent so much time watching the clock that on one occasion was scolded as "the boy who wastes his time staring at the clock." So colossally boring were her classes that I have absolutely no recollection of what she taught. My friends tell me that it was math. Maybe so. To Lizzie fell the onerous task of informing us that one of my frequent playmates, Phillip Littlefield (who had been sick), had succumbed to a pernicious tumor. Stunned silence pervaded our homeroom because few if any of us had experienced so close at hand the death of one so young. It was in Lizzie Giles' homeroom 7A that my class got involved in the so-called "bundles for Britain" program. That was during the 1940/1941 school year, when Great Britain was suffering mightily from daily bombings by Hitler's Luftwaffe. Our task was to prepare boxes (i.e., "bundles") of items deemed to be in short supply, for use by the child to whom the box would eventually be delivered. I was assigned the task of assembling and packing the items for a boy, including a bar of soap, a comb, a jackknife, a handkerchief, some candy, a toothbrush, and other useful things. We knew that some children had been evacuated from targeted areas, and some even brought to the U.S., but many were spending their nights in bomb shelters where any sort of gift would be most welcome. This activity brought us closer to the reality of war, but it was later, when we began to purchase defense stamps, that the war became a daily concern. I can't remember when these stamps were first available for purchase, but certainly not later than the first half of $8^{th}$ grade. By December of that year, the U.S. was at war with Japan, Germany and Italy. We were told that each $500 worth of stamps would pay for a jeep, and all of us probably believed that jeeps were what our money was buying (instead of, for example, tanks, food, rifles, etc.).

Miss Maxim taught hygiene, which was heavy on functioning of bodily systems, and a great geography class which was, well, great! Today's television quiz shows are shocking evidence that few of today's young people (20's, 30's) have had much if any exposure to physical or economic geography, and I laud Miss Maxim for instilling in her students a lasting appreciation and knowledge of the subject.

Miss Cunneen taught English (not my favorite subject), and was mistress of the A-L homeroom for eighth graders. Among other efforts, we had to learn all the parts of speech – adverbs, conjunctions, past participles, predicate adjectives, etc.– and how to parse a sentence. I never quite got the hang of all this, or understood why such exercises were necessary. Ignorance of such matters probably shows up in my writing, but I leave the reader to judge.

Room 8B was the homeroom of Miss Doris Walker, who taught science and did it very well. For the biology part of her course we dissected animals which had been pickled in formaldehyde, and I remember cutting open an earthworm, locust, and a frog. She sparked interest in what would become my bachelor's and doctoral degree minors!

Art classes were a mixed bag. During 8th grade, we learned all about mechanical drawing using T-square, triangles, ruler, drafting pencils, etc. Depicting three dimensional objects, learning about vanishing lines, and drawing plan views were skills we could utilize for a lifetime. Hat's off to you on that one, Miss Rowell. In the 7th grade, however, we got to express ourselves artistically, and for one project I drew and then painted a sunken pirate ship. With planked hull, high aftercastle, and broken rigging, the ship looked pretty realistic. Horizontal lines with a slight squiggle simulated current action, which was evident also in leaning strands of kelp. A human skeleton lay stretched on the sea floor. With watercolors, I painted the background a pale sea green, and painted the broken masts and yardarms brown. For the hull, I chose a sort of pale brownish orange color. Thoroughly satisfied that my painting was the result of artistic genius, I proudly submitted the finished work to Miss Rowell for approval. Well! She was disgusted! She railed at me for using such an outrageous color for the ship; crestfallen, I slunk back to my seat. She wouldn't even let me keep that undoubted masterwork! Years later, at Brixham, England, and on a nearby tidal flat, I spied two reproductions of 16th century ships that had been constructed for a movie about Sir Francis

Drake's defeat of the Spanish Armada. Color of the hulls? A sort of pale brownish orange, of course!

Foremost in my memory of 9th grade is the Latin class of Coach Stewart (behind his back he bore the name "Eddie"). A coach! Teaching Latin? I can remember the horror of noun declension, which to my un-nimble brain was far more difficult to grasp than verb conjugation. Declension of one pronoun goes: hic, haec, hoc, hujus, hujus, hujus (Eddie referred to the last three as "hujus throughout.") In fact, these are about the only words I can recall from that class. For oral tests, Eddie divided the class into teams: Harborites, who were basically the kids who had gone to Jenkins Elementary School, and the Hinterlanders, who were mainly kids who had gone to Hatherly Elementary School. For the latter, Eddie might ask, "Litchfield, what is a third declension Latin noun for the word "circumnavigation." (This example may not be grammatically correct, but you get the idea.) For the Harborites, Eddie might ask, "Flaherty, who was the quarterback for Notre Dame last year?" None of this is my imagination at work. Coach Stewart was famous for this sort of thing, never expressing even slight contrition for the obvious unfairness of these quizzes. Unsurprisingly, we Hinterlanders usually won these farcical "tests."

*Tales of a New England Boyhood*

One of our all time favorite teachers was Mr. Samuelson (we called him "Sammy"), who directed the marching band and orchestra. These became fine organizations under his gifted leadership! In an effort to stimulate interest in band and orchestra, Sammy arranged with a purveyor of musical instruments to bring in an assortment of horns – trumpet, French horn, trombone, baritone, etc. – and proceeded to play each one in an amazing display of versatility. My interest was very high, and Sammy came to our home with a trumpet. When he mentioned the price, $50.00, it was plain from my mom's expression that it might as well have been $5000.00. The band and orchestra would just have to make do without me. Sammy successfully created a fine marching band, and an excellent orchestra, the repertoire of the latter including a stirring rendition of "In a Persian Market." Elements of the band played at certain dancing school events – Millie Wharf (an adult) on piano, Don McPherson on bass, Elden Meyers on drums, Chris Weeks on trombone, etc. (The etc. means I can't remember the others.) After Sammy left for greener pastures, the new instrumental musician was Mr. Don Leach. Without Mr. Samuelson's vibrancy, interest in the band lessened, and at one home basketball game only five or six bandsmen showed up, including Mr. Leach with his trumpet. The bass drum stood idle. I was operating the electric scoreboard, and during the halftime lull Mr. Leach came over and asked me to play the big drum. What a thrill. All I had to do is watch his hand and beat the thing in time with the music. This feat was carried out with considerable aplomb, and I even stopped drumming on cue. My first (and only) performance in a band was an undoubted masterpiece of musicianship!

Another of our teachers was Mr. Wilcox, who taught high school physics and chemistry. Physics was a hoot. We learned all about inclined planes, mechanical advantage, electricity and magnetism, and air pressure (using Magdeburg hemispheres) – magic which contributed greatly to fascination amongst class members. But it was in chemistry class that Mr. Wilcox ("Willie" Wilcox behind his back) hit his stride. Among the many experiments was generation of hydrogen gas by reacting hydrochloric acid with chips of zinc. The vessel was a corked Ehrlenmeyer flask fitted with thistle tube "entrance" and tapered exit nozzle. Willie poured acid down the thistle tube, and attempted to ignite the escaping hydrogen. With a resounding bang, the entire apparatus exploded, propelling the much-shortened thistle tube over our heads to the laboratory back wall, and other junk elsewhere. Fortunately, no one was injured. Unfazed, Cobby Swift calmly took command of the situation by asking if he might have the broken thistle tube. A relieved Mr. Wilcox allowed that he might. Despite his occasional outbursts, such as, "____, how can you be so stupid?," Mr. Wilcox got high approval ratings amongst my classmates, and we chose him as our senior class advisor. For many years that role had been played by Miss Bessie M. Dudley, our high school English teacher, and she was not a little upset to be replaced by this relatively new member of the faculty.

In Miss Dudley's class, we read (or were supposed to have read) numerous classical pieces of literature, and also gave at least one book report each term. Strangely, some of the books I least enjoyed are today among my all-time favorites, especially *Silas Marner*. Regarding book reports, I note that one of the raciest books of the mid-1940's was Erskin Caldwell's *God's Little Acre*. During one book-report session, Louis Cerilli was called upon and he announced that he would report on that book. Miss Dudley snapped, "Louis, sit down." Obviously, she knew the content, and one could only surmise that she had read the naughty book. Anyway, English was perhaps our least favorite class, and it turned out that if we senior boys signed up for glee club we would once each month be able to avoid English. All of us signed up!

Then there was Miss Gile, our senior-year civics teacher, who also served as our home room supervisor. Home room was called the "study hall," and was used by groups other than ours, but the desks in that room contained *our* books and *our* supplies. We were arranged alphabetically in columns, from front to rear. I sat behind a feisty redhead named Ann Graham. Ornery kid that I tended to be, I tormented Ann by occasionally poking her in the back with a sharp pencil or pen point, and once even dropped a pinch of itching powder down her back. One morning, when I arrived at study hall, Ann was seated at *my* desk and Miss Gile indicated that I should sit at Ann's. Throughout the day, whenever our class was in study hall, Ann poked me with pencils and pen point, occasionally causing me to let out a loud, "ouch," or, "ow." Miss Gile paid absolutely no attention to these disruptions. My lesson learned, I never again troubled Miss Graham. Today, she is a close friend, but claims that a piece of pencil lead embedded in her back was emplaced there all those years ago by a very bad boy!

Civics class (read, "U.S. History") was as tedious as the name implies, one assignment being preparation of a concise outline of the Civil War. On this subject the chapter was ponderously full of dates, battles, and generals' names, so the task was as daunting as it was dull. To work on this, Cobby Swift and I teamed up in his living room, and after each of us had written two or three pages, we conspired to summarize our week's activities in explanation of our failure to complete the job. We pleaded that on Sunday evening we attended Christian Endeavor, Monday night was for Boy Scouts, Tuesday night was occupied by dancing school, and so on through the week, with Saturday night being "date night." Only Wednesday evening was available for homework, and we couldn't possibly finish the assignment in one night. We guessed that Miss Gile would not read beyond the first page or two of these reports. Boy! Were we wrong. The day after our reports were submitted, Miss Gile cornered me and made clear, in no uncertain terms, that the assignment was to be carried out in full, and there would be a stiff penalty for tardiness. Meany!

One day, a couple of the boys (*not* including me) in our civics class drummed up the idea of placing upended thumb tacks on Miss Gile's desk chair. They reasoned that she would not notice, because when entering the room she invariably walked straight to the desk and stood behind it while making announcements. I knew that Miss Gile was going to sit on those tacks, and that when she jumped up afterward I would probably have difficulty suppressing laughter. Had this happened, she immediately would have suspected my complicity. Not wishing to be implicated, I asked to be excused to answer a supposed call of nature. She gave permission, so I went to the locker room and waited 5 minutes before returning. The class was sitting in utter silence and Miss Gile was seated at her desk with tears in her eyes. She had been betrayed, not to say physically harmed, and doubtless was at the lowest ebb of her career. On that day, we all learned one of life's important lessons, and emotionally joined Miss Gile in her suffering.

Miss Harrington taught French, and all college and scientific course kids had to take three years of that language. Among our first sentences were "J'entre dans la salle de class," and "Je dit bonjour le professeur," and "Je prend ma place," and "Je prend le livre," and "J'ouvre le livre," and "Je regardez la page," etc. It was in this class that boredom led Dick Flaherty and me to concoct codes and send secret messages to one another. On one occasion, a class member walked into the classroom behind Miss Harrington and discreetly hung on her sweater a sign which read "Wolfess at Work." When she turned to the blackboard, the entire class broke into laughter. Guessing the cause, she removed the sign, but failed see the humor in this. A daily exercise was for each of us to say, in French, a common English word. When Louis Cerilli was asked to stand and recite the French word for vegetables (les legumes), he did not know the correct word, but gave it his best shot and said, "Les vegetables"

(Lay vej-a-tahb). In a curt voice, Miss H. requested that he sit down and henceforth spend more time on his assignments.

Our cafeteria was outfitted with square four-person tables and accompanying straight-backed chairs. Some students bought hot lunches, but most of my compatriots brought lunches from home. "P" Miles brought such exotic fare as puff-ball sandwiches, and one friend occasionally brought spinach sandwiches. Most others brought normal kinds of sandwiches – bologna, PB and J, etc. Lunch bringers still went through the "line," purchasing such necessities as small cartons of milk (cokes were not offered) and 5¢ packages of Hunt's potato chips. Our mundane conversations rarely concerned girls, and until partway through 11$^{th}$ grade I had had no interest in them. So, it came as no surprise when one day I overheard Betty Ann "Wiggly" Welch remark to her companions, "I think Donald Hattin is the most unromantic boy in this school." Whether or not she intended for me to hear this, my dates with Margie Macy later in the year may have prompted Betty Ann to change her mind. I hoped so.

During WWII, Eddie Stewart left for the U.S. Navy and was replaced (not the proper word) by Mr. Felix Dixon. Dixon was a huge man who had played football professionally, and was well liked by his students. At some point in each class meeting (my yearbook says he taught science), he found some reason to state, "If you give them an inch, they'll take 16 miles." "Them" included anyone who, or any group which, had somehow stepped out of line. Apparently, Felix believed it was his duty to admonish any kind of waywardness and to ensure that we must toe the mark.  Mr. Dixon was coach when I went out for football in my senior year. Not having the money for football shoes (it was either $10 or $20), I borrowed a pair from Pete Fleming, who had come down with an illness (mono?) as the season started. Pete's old shoes had worn-out cleats, and the sole of one shoe was broken across the arch area. I drilled holes on either side of the break, and stitched the two halves together with strong cotton cord. I bought one new cleat and proceeded to grind off about half so that it would match the others on the shoe for which it was intended. When uniforms were passed out, I got a pretty neat pair of pants which had built-in hip padding; however, "Buttons" Ewell asked me to trade with him because he was a running back and needed less cumbersome equipment. The strap-on type hip pads were old, sweat-stained, and bulky, but no matter, they served the purpose. That year, first-string players received bright new jerseys (rayon, I think), but I was assigned an old, faded, itchy woolen jersey which bore the number "15." We were so short of helmets that a substitute player (me) would take the helmet of whichever player he was replacing, regardless of whether or not it fit. During one practice I subbed for Billy Vining, whose helmet was way too big for me. On one play, as defensive left tackle, I took off after ball carrier Vinnie Dunphy, and lost my helmet several yards before bringing him down after a 30-yard gain. In those days, we didn't even use protective cups or mouth guards, and only one helmet, David Schultz's, had a face guard. When fully suited up, I looked a little bigger than my 135-pound weight would suggest, so on the dittoed game programs Felix listed me at 165 pounds. Similarly, he boosted the weight of all the other players. I didn't get to play in the first two games, the second involving a disastrous defeat (25-0) by the much heavier Class C team (Scituate was Class D) at Barnstable. My opportunity came during our third game. With Scituate ahead of Kingston 25-0, and time ready to expire, Felix put in No. 15 for the final play. As the ball was snapped, I shoved aside the opposing tackle, but was neatly upended by an alert halfback. This was my first (and only) moment of football glory. After another game, Pete Fleming had recovered from his illness and reclaimed his shoes. Without proper footgear, and the season half gone, I decided not to squander my slender resources on equipment which most likely would see only sideline action. As luck would have it,

Pete decided that his old worn-out shoes were, in fact, worn out, so he bought a new pair!

Basketball results were no better. Practices were exhilarating, and went well, but far too many kids were vying for permanent slots on the varsity team. During the last practice before our first game, which was an away game, Dixon posted names of those who would go on the bus and those who would not. My name was on neither list. I got the message, and opted instead to join the cheerleading squad. My high school athletic career was over.

About the most demeaning thing that could happen to a high school lad was to have his birthday remembered by his "buddies." In an action intended to humiliate the recipient, these friends would grab the celebrant and rush him to the boys locker room. Unceremoniously, three or four lads would upend the unfortunate birthday boy, lower his head into a toilet bowl, and push down on the flush lever. Imagining this treatment to be horrendously unpleasant, not to say unsanitary, I was careful on my 17th birthday to go repeatedly to the toilet area and flush the bowls over and over again so as to ensure the greatest possible degree of cleanliness in the event of a dunking. No one remembered my birthday, and I did not receive the otherwise obligatory shampoo.

Speaking of the restroom, I remember that the sink was partially walled off from the main area; while washing up one day, I heard voices coming through the wall from the girl's locker room. At the same time, several of the guys had lit some cigarettes – a not uncommon violation of administrative edicts. While I strained to hear what the girls were saying, our principal, Mr. Parkhurst, burst into the room and put a quick end to the nicotine-motivated transgressions. Sheepishly, I stepped out of the sink area, whereupon Mr. Parkhurst glared at me and snapped, "Donald Hattin, *Boy Scout*!" Naively, I assumed he knew about my "listening in," and only later realized that he was lumping me with the sneaky smokers. Taking this false rap was a bitter pill, indeed, because whatever esteem he may have held for me dropped that day to an all-time low. I should have stayed hidden in the sink area!

Each year, high schoolers put on two plays – the all-school play and the senior-class play. November 16, 1945, marked not only my 17th birthday, but also my stage debut. Entitled *The Showboat Minstrels*, and directed by Miss Gile, the performance included songs, dancing and instrumental music. Louis Cerilli and Annelaine Limper sang a superb duet. A barbershop number was performed by the Boll Weevil Quartet, featuring Don McPherson, "P" Miles, "Twit" Swift and me. The minstrel part of show included Don McPherson as interlocutor and several actors in blackface, myself included. After the play, which was an unqualified success, I hoped to see my girlfriend, Margie Macy, but removal of the greasepaint took more than half an hour, by which time she had long since departed for home. Anticipated accolades never came from that quarter.

Our senior class play, performed on April 26, 1946, was entitled *Strictly Formal*, and was the story of teenagers and their dating problems. Several actors were miscast, especially "P" Miles, who played the unlikely role of a shot-putting athlete despite the fact of his slightly built frame. With a pretty dull plot and mostly wooden acting, the evening was salvaged by our glee club, and by one actor who used the word "hell" (the

Pete Fleming signing Margie Macy's yearbook on Class Day, 1946.

script called for "hell") instead of "heck," as instructed. As a character named "Jim," I played what was supposed to be a quasi-romantic role in a most unromantic fashion, thus ending a wholly unpromising stage career.

Graduation from high school, as with most such affairs, was an event marked by moments of sadness, nostalgia, joy and pain. On Wednesday, June 12, 1946, our class paraded onto the stage to the tune of Elgar's classic *Pomp and Circumstance*, played by the school orchestra. Pete Fleming, class president, gave the address of welcome, which was followed by presentation of prizes and scholarships. This was an arena occupied by serious students. Expectably, my name was unmentioned. Musical entertainment comprised a choral number performed by our class and the school chorus, accompanied by the school orchestra. For reasons known only to her, our vocal music teacher had selected *Bells* by Sergei Rachmaninoff. Except for the well-known funeral march itself, no composition in our knowledge sounded so funereal. Shortly after we had begun practicing this depressing piece, Pete told Miss Reynolds that our class objected to including same in the graduation ceremony. Looking hurt, she replied that no change could be made because the programs were already being printed. (*So,* just tell the audience that a change has been made!) In the event, we

Donald E. Hattin

Scituate High School class of 1946.

started singing this mournful dirge in the four-part harmony that had been practiced and practiced, but soon all of us gave up and sang only the melody. The whole thing was a disaster, and I can still hear that mass of untutored voices struggling valiantly to an agonizing conclusion. Miss Reynolds' folly was more than compensated by presentation of diplomas by the School Committee Chairman, Mr. Thomas W. Macy, father of my sweetheart. With a presence that belied his lack of a high school diploma, he remarked that he had known many of these kids for most of their lives, and that they had, "tramped mud into my living room, drunk my coca colas, and eaten all my potato chips, but if they hadn't, my house wouldn't be a home." He really meant that. Hearing it brought tears to my eyes, and doubtless to the eyes of many others. Diploma conferral was followed by the class ode, sung to the tune "Memories," with words by Louis Cerilli and Bob Holcomb. Then we marched out. Our class numbered 47 students – 30 girls and 17 boys. In 2006, we will gather in Scituate once again, to celebrate our 60th class reunion!

# Chapter 20
# End Of The Beginning

Following my first summer of work in the fields for Ben Meyers, I embarked on an adventure which would shape my life for many decades to come. In September, 1946, I packed clothing, sheets, blankets, towels and other gear into the same steamer trunk that my mother had used when she went off to Brown University more than thirty years earlier, and shipped it via Railway Express to Butterfield House at Massachusetts State College.[1] A few days later, carrying only a small suitcase, and armed with a few dollars in spending money, I took a train from North Scituate to Boston's South Station, and traveled thence to the city of Springfield, MA, on a diesel-powered train of sleek aluminum coaches. En route, I met two or three fellows who within a few days would become campus classmates, and whose instant friendship eliminated any misgivings I may have had about leaving home for a protracted period of time unaccompanied by parents. At Springfield, a change of trains brought a huge surprise, on which I look back with great nostalgia. From

---

[1] Within months the name was changed to University of Massachusetts.

Springfield to Northampton we rode on a steam-hauled train of old-fashioned *wooden* coaches – wooden sides, wooden floors, wooden armrests. The air smelled of coal smoke, the floors were cindery, and the ride was slow and jouncy. I discovered that these ancient coaches were referred to as B&M (Boston and Maine) "boxcars," and they were really quite wonderful.

From Northampton our trip continued by bus and cab to the lovely campus which would be my home for much of the next four years. That fall, on November 16, I reached the age of 18. My boyhood had ended, and so has this book.

Fini